THE UNIVERSITY PITT CLUB

WALTER MORLEY FLETCHER

President 1899–1914

THE
UNIVERSITY PITT CLUB

1835—1935

By
WALTER MORLEY FLETCHER
Sometime President

Completed by
CHARLES MONTAGUE FLETCHER

CAMBRIDGE

PRINTED FOR THE CLUB AT THE
UNIVERSITY PRESS

1935

CAMBRIDGE UNIVERSITY PRESS
Cambridge, New York, Melbourne, Madrid, Cape Town,
Singapore, São Paulo, Delhi, Tokyo, Mexico City

Cambridge University Press
The Edinburgh Building, Cambridge CB2 8RU, UK

Published in the United States of America by Cambridge University Press, New York

www.cambridge.org
Information on this title: www.cambridge.org/9781107600065

First published 1935
First paperback edition 2011

A catalogue record for this publication is available from the British Library

ISBN 978-1-107-60006-5 Paperback

CONTENTS

ILLUSTRATIONS

PLANS

PREFACE

THE UNIVERSITY PITT CLUB has entered upon its hundredth year. That fact furnishes an excuse, of a kind universally accepted nowadays, for placing on record what is known of the beginnings and the growth of the institution.

Not that an excuse is very necessary. The Pitt Club has a strong hold upon the affection of its members past and present. It has always been a place for the making and strengthening of friendships, and in recent years its amenities have been most notably increased: but at no time during my acquaintance with it could an inquirer have gathered much knowledge about it. Its undergraduate members have accepted and enjoyed the advantages it offers, but very few of them could ever have told you why it was called the Pitt Club, or where its abode had been, or indeed, any single fact in its story. I cannot, however, doubt that they will be glad to have that story told in the vivid fashion in which it appears in these pages. It will also come as a surprise to them (though to a slightly older generation it will not) to learn what an enormous proportion of its growth and of its comforts the Club owes to one man—Sir Walter Fletcher. As Mr E. M. Clark has very truly written: "The name of the original founder of the University Pitt Club has unfortunately not survived: but the Club had a second founder, whose name should never be forgotten—Walter Morley Fletcher." Besides the material improvements which Sir Walter carried through, the Club is in his debt for the conception, and a great part of the writing, of this history which his death in 1933 did not permit him to complete. The lines of it had been laid out by him with the clearness which marked all his work; and his handling of the subject shows his remarkable capacity for interesting himself and others in matters which one would have said were remote from his ordinary avocations. Yet to any one who knew him it will seem natural that he should spend time and labour—and not a little of it—in lengthy and minute gathering and verifying of the facts and reminiscences which he has put together here. The result, to which others have made valuable contributions (as is recorded by Mr Francis Clark) is a thoroughly adequate, scholarly, and readable history. I have no hesitation in using these laudatory words, for I am innocent of any share in the composition. But I cordially welcome the record, and am convinced that the younger public to whom it is directly addressed will welcome it likewise. In my own undergraduate days the Pitt, undisturbed as it was by politics and debates, was a delightful refuge, even with its very modest capacities for nourishing the bodies and minds of its members. Now that it can do so much more for them, their gratitude and their pride in it must be more lively than ever.

M. R. JAMES

The Lodge
Eton College
July 1935

INTRODUCTION

THIS HISTORY would not be complete without a word as to its writing and its writers.

It is in the main the work of Sir Walter Fletcher. He had himself begun a preface which throws light on his sources and methods, and suggests that the idea of a history of the Club occurred to him almost as soon as he became its President. It is only a fragment, but is worth quoting in full:

"For many years both the age and historical origin of the U.P.C. have been involved in doubt. When I succeeded Dr James as President of the Club in 1899, the Annual List of members bore upon its cover in conspicuous type, and had borne for many years, the statement that the Club was 'founded in 1839'. From the oldest resident members of the Club, Alfred Newton, Professor of Zoology—that peerless Sunday evening host—and Lord Braybrooke, Master of Magdalene, I gathered in many happy and well-remembered conversations their reminiscences of the Club from their own days, but those were far from the Club's beginning. I found it generally believed that the Club had originated as a Tory dining Club to keep warm the memory of Mr William Pitt and that it had gradually lost its politics as it acquired Club rooms and so developed into its present state.

"Nothing appeared however to justify the supposed foundation in 1839. Search in the Club's archives revealed at once a list of members beginning from October 1835."

The written material available for Sir Walter Fletcher consisted of the list of members to which he refers, and records of Committee meetings and financial transactions. He also drew on the recollections of those who had known the Club in its early days, thus preserving incident and reminiscence which would otherwise have been lost.

At the time of his death in 1933 he had carried the history of the Club up to 1887, the date of the election of Dr James as President.

The work could not be left unfinished. Two of Sir Walter Fletcher's successors as President were ready to give their help. Mr Edward Mellish Clark provided material relating to the years when he was Treasurer (1905–20) and President (1920–29), and having taken an active part in the execution of the important structural changes of his time, he has been able to ensure the accuracy of the plans of the Club buildings at the various stages in their development. These plans are the gift of Mr C. W. Long, the Club's architect.

Sir Stephen Gaselee has given help and information for the various periods of which he had special knowledge—of 1900–04 when he was an undergraduate member, of 1904–05 when he served on the Committee, of 1914–19 when he was President, and the production and appearance of this history owe much to his advice.

Mr E. M. Clark and Sir S. Gaselee between them could thus recount the greater part of the history left unwritten by Sir Walter Fletcher. But someone was wanted to co-ordinate what they had written and to bring the story up to date.

Most fortunately Mr Charles Fletcher was on the spot ready to take up the pen. He was elected a member of the Club in 1930, came on to the Committee in 1931, and was Secretary 1932–33. Thus he had first-hand knowledge of the later years. And more, as son of Sir Walter Fletcher, he knew his father's plans, had possession of his father's material, and was in touch with his father's friends, Mr E. M. Clark and Sir S. Gaselee. He was therefore the right person to put the history in its final form. This he has done. Present and future members of the University Pitt Club will be grateful to him and his collaborators for completing the work that will always be connected with the name of Sir Walter Fletcher.

I would like to add that the records of the Club are being well and carefully kept. The historians of our second century should find their task made easy.

F. H. H. CLARK
President U.P.C.

Magdalene College
July 1935

THE UNIVERSITY PITT CLUB

I

PITT CLUBS, AND THE FOUNDATION OF THE UNIVERSITY PITT CLUB AT CAMBRIDGE IN 1835

THE life of the University Pitt Club at Cambridge began in the Michaelmas Term of 1835. We have the original roll of members, more than a hundred in that first term, without any indication of the names or purposes of either the begetters of the Club or its first leaders. But we have Minutes of the meetings from 1838 onwards, and from those, with the help of other evidence, we learn that the Club was founded to do honour to the name and memory of Mr William Pitt, to uphold in general the political principles for which he stood, and in particular to assist the local party organisations of the town of Cambridge to return worthy, that is to say, Tory, representatives to Parliament and to the Borough Council. According to the fashion of the times these political activities were combined with the pleasures of social intercourse at dinner, when party fervour among friends, dining in party uniform, might be warmed towards a political incandescence by the speeches to successive toasts.

The very fact that the Club appears to have sprung at a bound into active life and numerous membership suggests some relationship to the system of Pitt Clubs which had spread throughout the country a quarter of a century earlier. We have no direct evidence of any such relationship, but it may have existed, and some account therefore of the earlier Pitt Clubs will not be out of place.

Within the first years after the death of William Pitt,[1] organisations called "Pitt Clubs" came into being in almost every part of the country. These were devoted to the tasks of keeping alive his fame by regular commemoration, and of using his name and example as rallying cries in the interests of the Tory party. In 1808 the central "Pitt Club" of London, under the presidency of the Duke of Richmond, supported by a noble and distinguished body of vice-presidents, held the first "Triennial Commemoration of the Anniversary of Mr Pitt's Birth" in the form of a great Banquet at the Merchant Taylors' Hall, and this was repeated thereafter at intervals of three years. By 1817, when the fourth Triennial Commemoration was held in the same Hall, among the seventeen standing toasts, of the usual loyal, patriotic, and political kinds that were drunk (together with five "occasional" toasts), the toast list included the toasts not only of the London Pitt Club itself, but also of "the Duke of Buccleugh and the Pitt Club of Scotland" and of "Lord Kenyon and the Pitt Club of Wales". By that time there had been formed in England the Pitt Clubs of Devon and Exeter, Manchester, Bolton, Blackburn,

---

[1] Born May 28th, 1759; died January 23rd, 1806.

2

Warrington, Birmingham, Wolverhampton, North Staffordshire, Leicestershire and Leicester, Doncaster, Halifax, Leeds, Scarborough, Sheffield, Hampshire, Norwich, Reading, Taunton and Somersetshire, Northumberland and Newcastle-upon-Tyne, North and South Shields, Nottingham, Carlisle, Liverpool, Hereford, Bristol and Derby. In Wales, besides the Pitt Club of Wales, there was the Menai Pitt Club meeting at Caernarvon.

All these Clubs appear to have held anniversary dinners upon the 28th of May, the birthday of Mr Pitt, when his "immortal memory" might be drunk in pious silence and the enthusiasm of the local Tory interests kept alive. Privileges of affiliation were given them by the central Pitt Club, London, and members of local Pitt Clubs "on the Production of a Certificate of their Qualification" might be admitted extraordinary members of it on suitable payment, and might "attend the monthly and Anniversary Dinners, when in Town, on payment of the usual Charge for Non-Subscribers' Tickets, and appearing with a Medal of the Country Club to which they belong".

Of all these local Pitt Clubs many died out within a generation, and few, if any, now survive. The parent Pitt Club still meets annually in London and renews its past at dinner, though with a greatly shortened toast list. One of the extinct country Pitt Clubs, that of Northumberland and Newcastle-upon-Tyne, has gained a posthumous recognition of a curiously accidental kind. For each of the annual Commemorations held by this

Club, and probably first for that of 1815, Thomas Bewick of Newcastle provided a fine woodcut of the crest, arms and motto of Mr Pitt to adorn an octavo pamphlet giving the list of officers and members of the Club with the words of the songs and glees to be performed at the Birthday Dinner. Copies of these pamphlets are "items" of interest for collectors of Bewick woodcuts and they are by no means common. This accident of decoration has led no doubt to the preservation of copies that would otherwise have disappeared. Each Commemoration pamphlet gives an account of the proceedings at the Dinner of the preceding year, and the following description of the festivities of May 28th, 1818, from the Club pamphlet for 1819, may probably be taken as fairly representative of similar celebrations by other local Pitt Clubs and of the enthusiasms of that earlier generation of diners. It shows at least what a hardy race these northerners were.

On Thursday, May 28th, 1818, the Northumberland and Newcastle upon Tyne Pitt Club celebrated, according to custom, the anniversary of the birth of the late illustrious statesman the Right Honourable William Pitt, by a grand dinner at the Assembly Rooms, Newcastle. The assemblage, on the occasion, comprehended a large portion of gentlemen of leading rank and opulence in the county and neighbourhood, and the number that sat down to dinner, including visitors, was about 62.

The President for the year, Thomas Clennell, Esq. of Harbottle Castle, was in the chair, supported on the right by the High-Sheriff of Northumberland, and on the left by Sir Charles Loraine, Bart. John Reed, Esq. of Chipchase, and William Orde, Esq. of Nunnykirk, did the honours as

4

vice-presidents, at the two extremities of the table at the lower end of the room.

The members appeared with their medals, and the stewards were distinguished by rosettes also; a full band of music was in attendance, and enlivened the scene with appropriate pieces.

The proceedings of the day were most ably conducted by the president, and we can give only a faint outline of the language and energy with which the various toasts were introduced by him.

The first toast was, of course, the king, and the President gave it in the following emphatic words: "Our highly respected and venerable King, the early patron of Mr Pitt." Drank with three times three cheers, accompanied with thunders of applause, and the music of *God save the King*, by the band. The next toast was,—"The Prince Regent, who has rendered himself illustrious and beloved, by adopting the principles, and following the measures of his Father." Three times three. Music—*The Prince Regent's March.* "The Queen, and better health to her." Music— *Here's a Health to all good Lassies.* "The Duke of York, and the other branches of the Royal Family." Three times three. Music—*The Duke of York's March.*

The President then rose and addressed the meeting in a short but elegant eulogium on Mr Pitt, and prefatory to the toast of the day. He said it was customary for persons placed in the situation where he was, and in which he felt great pleasure, to say a few words on the subject of the meeting; but having been from his earliest life a warm and constant admirer of Mr Pitt and his principles, and now addressing a meeting who knew so well how to appreciate them, he deemed only a few words necessary. He observed of Mr Pitt, that, tracing his origin from his great and illustrious father, and blending what he learnt from him with his own capacious mind and wonderful endowments, he was, by education and descent, at once the child and the patriot of his country, and concluded by giving as a toast, "The immortal memory of the late Right Honourable William Pitt!" The toast was drank with reverential silence, and followed by the performance, by the band, of the grand and solemn music from *The Overture to Artaxerxes*.

The next toast was,—"The House of Brunswick, and may they never forget the principles which seated them on the throne of these realms."

The President then rose, and, adverting to the heavy loss the country had sustained by the death of the late lamented her Royal Highness the Princess Charlotte of Wales, on whose excellence and virtues, and to whose character and conduct, in every point of view, sufficient praise and veneration could never be given, begged, as the only tribute we could now bestow, to give, as a toast,— "The revered memory of the late lamented Her Royal Highness the Princess Charlotte of Wales! And may her virtues long live in the remembrance of her country!" This was also drank with perfect and reverential silence, and followed by the music of *The Dead March in Saul*. The next toast was,—"The late Marriages and the intended Marriages of the Royal Family, and success to them; and whenever an heir is born, may it inherit not only the crown but the virtues of its ancestors", 3 times 3. Music—*Haste to the Wedding*. "The present Ministry, and may the principles of Mr Pitt ever animate their councils", 3 times 3.

Mr Orde, vice-president, rose, and recurring to the lamented death of the Princess Charlotte, and recollecting what must be the grief of her survivors, proposed as a toast,—"His Royal Highness Prince Leopold", with 3 times 3. Drank with great applause.

The President then gave,—"Field-Marshal His Grace the Duke of Wellington and his Army, and when they retire from service, may they completely enjoy domestic happiness", with 3 times 3. Music—*He was famed for deeds of arms*. "The Pilot that weather'd the storm." "The

6

High Sheriff for the county of Northumberland", with 3 times 3. The High Sheriff returned his thanks, and proposed the "Health of the President, together with the Bench of Magistrates of Northumberland", drank with 3 times 3. The President, as a magistrate, returned thanks, and drank "The Company's good health"; to which Mr Orde added, "and may they long see us magistrates, and may we long drink their healths." "The Conservatorship of the River Tyne, and High Water Mark". "The Coal Trade." "The Lord Lieutenant of the county of Northumberland." "The Stewards of the Club, and thanks to them for their services." Thanks returned by Colonel Reed, who proposed, as a toast,—"May we long live to meet upon this occasion."

The President then gave the "Health of Mr Orde, Vice-President", with 3 times 3.

Mr Orde rose to return thanks, and to address the meeting; he regretted that urgent and important private business in London had caused him to be absent from the last anniversary of this Club, especially as they had done him the honour to elect him their president for that occasion; but he trusted they would not impute to him any dereliction either of his duty or his attachment to the memory and principles of Mr Pitt, which he held in the highest veneration and regard. Mr Orde then entered on an animated panegyric of the transcendant abilities of that great statesman, whose image, he said (pointing to a bust of Mr Pitt, which stood on the mantle piece in the room), brought strongly to his recollection many instances of the surprising energy of mind, and extraordinary powers of eloquence, displayed by that great man, to which he had himself been an admiring witness. A sudden indisposition here seized Mr Orde, and rendered him unable to proceed; he sat down evidently under great uneasiness, and was advised to go into another room for a while, which he did, and although he soon returned to his seat at the table, somewhat recovered, yet he continued the remainder of the evening under great uneasiness and depression.

The President next gave—"Ships, colonies, and commerce." Sir Charles Loraine then proposed the "Health of Colonel Clennell, as president of the Pitt Club", which was drank with 3 times 3, and much applause. Mr Clennell returned his heartfelt thanks for the honour done him, by their having chosen him president, and said, he had always been an advocate for Mr Pitt, and was glad of every opportunity to pay tribute to his memory and his measures; and added, he trusted that those principles which had carried us through the French revolution, would always carry us into the harbour of peace. The next toast was, "The gentlemen of the committee", for which suitable thanks were returned by Mr John Lambton Loraine, the Rev. Mr Blackburn, Mr Askew, and others.

Mr Orde, after apologizing for his temporary absence, occasioned by indisposition, and agitation of spirits, rose to offer his congratulations to the town of Newcastle, on the number of great men that had sprung from thence, and whose talents and services to their country, in various ways, had done honour to their native town; and, alluding to one man, whose great and extensive learning, whose inflexible integrity and loyalty, joined to his long association with, and steady adherence to, Mr Pitt and his principles, intitled him to the admiration and regard of his country, and especially of his townsmen, proposed the "Health of John Lord Eldon, Lord High Chancellor of England". This toast was drank with 3 times 3, and followed with long and incessant applause.

After five more toasts of a personal kind, the account continues:

Mr Orde then proposed, as a toast, a sentiment, which, he said, originated, and was a favourite, with Mr Pitt himself,—"The Rights of the Crown, and the Liberties of the People; may we be equally ready to maintain the one and to assert the other."

Mr Orde next proposed "The non-members or visitors,

8

who had this day honoured the Pitt Club with their company." The President gave "Colonel Lord Lovaine and the Northumberland Militia", with 3 times 3. Lieut. Col. Coulson returned thanks. Mr Vicar proposed the "Health of the Secretary to the Club", Mr Thomas Brown, "with thanks for his services". Mr Brown returned thanks.

Then followed no less than twenty more toasts, including "The Land we live in, and may those who don't like it, leave it"; "Lord Lascelles, and the parent Pitt Club of England"; "Both sides of the Tweed"; "The Navy" (music and chorus, *Rule Britannia*); "The royal wreath, the Rose, the Thistle, the Shamrock and the Leek"; "The trade and port of Newcastle" (music, *Weel may the keel row*).

The President then rose and addressed the company again, and, after thanking them for the honour they had done him, and the zeal they had shewn for the promotion and support of the principles for which the club was instituted, begged leave to give, as a toast, "The next meeting", and, having drank it, retired amidst loud plaudits.

Colonel Reed was then called to the chair, and continued to keep up the festivity of the occasion till a late hour. Several more toasts followed, among which were the following:—By Mr Adamson, "Success to the expedition to the North Pole". By Lieut. Henry Clayton, "The Duke of York and the army", with 3 times 3. By Col. Reed, "The Plough, the Fleece, and the Sail". With several others.

In the course of the evening several songs were sung, and all persons present seemed to vie with each other in supporting and maintaining the spirit and conviviality of the meeting, and the loyal and patriotic "PITT" principle on which this society was established, and on which it rests, and looks for support and perpetuity.

The support and perpetuity for which this convivial meeting looked so ardently do not appear to have been realised, for this series of commemorations at New-castle-on-Tyne came to an end in 1823.

It is a matter for some surprise that in neither of the Universities of Oxford or Cambridge, nor in the Boroughs or Counties in which they are situated, was there any Pitt Club founded during the period when Tories were so ready to form them. William Pitt had been educated at Pembroke College, Cambridge, and at the time of his death was Chancellor of the University. The University made permanent memorials of his name and fame by erecting a statue to him in the Senate House and by associating his name for ever with the University Press. It is probable that the early foundation of the Pitt Club in London met the desires of those seniors in Cambridge who from party ties or motives of personal piety sought more active and convivial commemoration. It may be noted that the "Worshipful the Vice-Chancellor of the University of Cambridge" figured as one of the Stewards of the third triennial dinner held by the Pitt Club in London on May 28th, 1814.

The University Pitt Club at Cambridge was from the first, and has always remained, an undergraduate organisation. It sprang into full life, as we have seen, in the Michaelmas Term of 1835. The first list of members bears that date and every subsequent term up to the present has its formal record of added members. From the first, and throughout the century of life it has now completed, it has always used the initials "U.P.C." and has never followed the practice of other clubs here, whether political or athletic, of specifying its University as being that of Cambridge. It is uncertain whether this is because the Club is the only University Club dedicated to Pitt or because it regards Cambridge as the only University. The first list of members shows that the earliest membership was well distributed throughout the University, if we allow for the great predominance in members that Trinity and St John's had at that time. It contains the names of 113 undergraduates with that of one bachelor of arts. Of these, 67 were members of Trinity, 21 were of St John's, while ten other colleges were represented by five members each or less. Within the first year every College in the University except Sidney Sussex was represented in the Club. The terminal subscription was one guinea.

Although since 1868, at latest, the Pitt Club has ceased from all political activity and has elected members to its social advantages without any regard whatever to considerations of political party, the tradition has always been preserved that the Club was originally formed to unite undergraduates attached to the Conservative party by birth or inclination, and to promote the party interests. It was natural that at Cambridge such a Club should rally under the name of Pitt, and although it was quite dissociated in time from the numerous Pitt Clubs that had been formed, as we have just seen, a quarter of a century earlier throughout the country, the convivial modes it adopted of commemorating Mr Pitt and of doing homage to sound Conservative principles by means of periodical dinners so well reflects the practice of the older Pitt Clubs as to suggest that the undergraduate founders were in some degree taking as their model what their fathers had formerly practised in the country or were still practising in London. Whether it was more than a political dining club at the beginning must remain quite uncertain. Within two or three years of its foundation, however, the Club took an active part, as we shall see, in assisting by direct financial subventions and otherwise the Conservative interest within the Borough of Cambridge.

Some relics piously collected after 1900, when the Club had long lost its strictly political and party leanings, have wholly confirmed, so far as they go, these historical traditions. Earliest of these is the form of receipt for a subscription paid to the University Pitt Club in the October Term 1835 by Mr R. Pollock, whose name stands 20th on the list of original members of the Club. The receipt form is marked as coming from "Volume I". This Mr R. Pollock was Robert John Pollock (Trinity College), the second of the twenty-four children of Jonathan Frederick Pollock, Fellow of Trinity College, 1807, Conservative member for Huntingdon from 1831, Attorney-General in both Sir Robert Peel's administrations (1834–5 and 1841–4). He became Chief Baron of the Exchequer in 1844, 1st Baronet in 1866 and died in 1870.

It was found among his papers by his grandson

Rivers Pollock (Trinity College, U.P.C. 1903), and given to the Club in 1905.

Some interesting information and records were obtained from Mr Francis Simpson (Queens' College, U.P.C. 1836), who was President of the Club in the Easter Term 1838, and was still alive in 1905, by his son Mr F. C. Simpson (Trinity College, U.P.C. 1865) and his grandson Mr W. A. Simpson (Trinity Hall, U.P.C. 1904). Mr Francis Simpson "well remembered his connection with the Pitt Club. It was started in his time". "It was the means of returning Conservative Members for the Town of Cambridge instead of Radicals." He had preserved some printed notices of summons to meetings of the Club. Each of these is a double sheet, printed on one side, and had been folded, wafered, 'and addressed on the outside. They bear dated Cambridge postmarks, but of course no postage stamps.

The earliest of them, dated April 18th, 1836, is in the following terms:

General Meeting of the University Pitt Club to be held at the Sun Hotel[1] on the following Thursday "at 12 noon precisely". The business is

The Election of a President.

The Election of Nine Members of Committee.

A motion on the subject of a Reading Room, by Mr BUDWORTH, *Jesus*, adjourned from last meeting.

[1] This stood opposite the Great Gate of Trinity. Its site was purchased by Dr Whewell, Master of Trinity, before 1850 with a view to the erection of the new Whewell's Court, long called "the Master's Court", which was begun in 1859 and completed in 1860.

The next, dated October 24th, 1836, is a similar notice for a general meeting to be held at the Red Lion Hotel on Thursday, October 27th, at half-past one o'clock, for the Election of President, Treasurer, Secretary and three new members of Committee. These notices are both signed by Mr Alexander Watson.

The last, undated but bearing postmark of November 22nd, 1836, is given in facsimile. This summons to Dinner makes the only known formal reference in the Club records to the uniform worn by the members in the early years of the Club.

Mr Francis Simpson remembered upon inquiry in 1905 that the uniform was a "chocolate coloured coat with buttons". He had kept a set of the Club buttons and gave these to his son when in 1865 he became a member in his turn. By that time all knowledge of the use of the uniform and buttons had died out. Mr F. C. Simpson presented one of the buttons to the Club in 1904. It bears the initials U.P.C. intertwined, and surmounted by a Royal Crown.

From the very few survivors of the earliest members of the Club, to whom inquiries were addressed after 1900, little information could be obtained beyond that which has already been given. The 7th Duke of Rutland (Trinity College, b. 1818, d. 1906), better known in political life as Lord John Manners, who was elected to the Club in his first term, Michaelmas 1836, wrote as follows in 1902:

I much regret my inability to throw any light on the questions connected with the history of the U.P.C. which

UNIVERSITY PITT CLUB.

SIR,

I beg to inform you that the MEMBERS of the UNIVERSITY PITT CLUB will dine together at the RED LION INN, on FRIDAY the 2nd of December. Dinner on the table at 6 o'clock precisely. Tickets to be had at the bar of the Inn; which you are requested to apply for three days before the Dinner.

I am, Sir,

Your obedient servant,

CHARLES TOWER,

Secretary.

N.B.—It is the particular request of the Committee that all Members will make a point of appearing in the Uniform of the Club.

you submit to me. When I went up to the University I found it in existence, joined it, and took part in its operations, whatever they were. The most active and influential member at that time was a Fellow Commoner of Corpus, by name Watson, who from his imposing personality, fluent speech and constant energy, was known as "Corpus of Watson".

Minutes of the Club proceedings have fortunately been preserved for the years 1838 to 1847 inclusive, and the earliest of these bring out clearly the political and social activities that doubtless had been the chief objects of the foundation of the Club in 1835. For the first time we have a full list of the Officers and Committee members.

Committee for Easter Term 1838

F. R. SIMPSON, Esq., Queens', *President.*
Sir J. H. LIGHTON, John's, *Secretary.*
H. BULLOCK, Esq., Christ's, *Treasurer.*

Lord JOHN MANNERS, Trinity.
Honble G. S. SMYTHE, John's.
Honble E. HERBERT, John's.
W. STIRLING, Esq., Trinity.
F. G. GREGOR, Esq., Trinity.
R. BATESON, Esq., Trinity.
F. GOULBURN, Esq., Trinity.
B. W. SAVILE, Esq., Emmanuel.
J. P. BUDWORTH, Esq., Jesus.
G. JACKSON, Esq., Magdalene.

The political activities of the U.P.C. can now be seen in some detail from the Minutes.

Committee meeting held at Mr Bullock's (Christ's) rooms on Monday the 7th May, 1838.

Ordered, That £8. 12s. 0d. be paid for the Standard newspaper and Conservative Journal to Thomas Kennedy for the use of the Operative Conservative Association of the town of Cambridge.

Committee meeting held at Mr Bullock's rooms on Saturday the 12th May, 1838.

In the absence of the late President (Mr Bateson) the chair was taken by Lord John Manners.

Mr Barker attended on behalf of the Cambridge Conservative Association on the subject of a debt amounting to £79. 8s. 0d., incurred by that society.

It was moved by Lord John Manners, and seconded by the Honble. G. Smythe, "That the whole debt be paid out of the funds of the club upon an understanding that an immediate report be presented to the committee by the managing body of the Association giving an account of its present prospects and resources. And also that a half-yearly report be presented in the first week of May and the first week of November." Carried unanimously.

Committee meeting held at Sir John Lighton's rooms on Monday, 5th November, 1838.

...Ordered, That £20 be given to the general Committee for promoting the election of Town Councillors in the late municipal elections to defray expenses incurred by them in those elections.

We can now learn more of the proceedings at the Club dinners. The toast list settled by the Committee, long as it seems to us now, must be regarded as being severely restrained if we compare it with the toast lists of Pitt Club dinners in other places, of which an earlier example has been given. Each member dining paid £1. 7s. 6d. as "Dinner Money".

Committee meeting held at Lord J. Manners's rooms on Wednesday the 14th November, 1838.

Voted that the Dinner take place on Thursday the 22nd Nov. at half past six o'clock.

The following toasts were arranged for the dinner:

1. The Queen.   *The President* (G. S. Smythe).
   [God save the Queen.]

2. The Queen Dowager and the rest of
   the Royal Family.   *The President.*
   [German Walze.]

3. Church and State.   *Hon. E. Herbert.*
   [Hallalujah Chorus.]

4. The Immortal Memory of Mr Pitt.   *J. B. Budworth.*
   [Silence.]

5. Army and Navy.   *Balfour (J.B.).*
   [Rule Britannia.]

6. Duke of Wellington.   *L. Jones.*
   [See the Conquering Hero come.]

7. Lord Lyndhurst and the House of
   Lords.   *Stokes.*
   [Auld Lang Syne.]

8. Sir R. Peel and the House of Com-
   mons.   *Stirling.*
   [Awa' Whigs awa'.]

9. Lord Stanley.   *Bateson.*
   [Ye Gentlemen of England.]

10. Chandos and Agriculture.   *Lord J. Manners.*
    [Speed the Plough.]

11. Sister University.   *Hope.*

12. The Yeomanry.   *Hon. E. Herbert.*

13. The Colonies and may they never be
    lost or given away.   *Sir S. Clarke.*

14. Justice to Ireland.   *Simpson.*

19

15. The President.
   [Jolly Good Fellow.]

16. Members for the University.   *Gregor.*

17. May England, etc.   *Savile.*

18. Success to U.P.C.   *Bullock.*
   [A Bumper of Burgundy.]

19. Cambridge Conservative Association and all similar associations throughout the country.   *Banton.*
   [Willie brew'd a peck o' Malt]

20. The strangers.

21. Our next merry meeting.   *The President.*
   [God save the Queen.]

In this list, printed here as it appears in the Minutes, have been inserted (in square brackets) the pieces of music accompanying the toasts, which are taken from an almost identical but undated toast list of the next year which was found with the Minutes. In the accounts it appears that at each of the dinners at this time Mr John Manning was paid four guineas for the Band.

Selected extracts may now be given in order from the Minutes.

Committee meeting held at F. Goulburn, Esq.'s rooms, Trinity, May 23rd, 1839.

Resolved, that the sum of £105 be placed by the Treasurer in the hands of G. Fisher on the *express stipulation* that if there be no contested election before the twenty-fourth of October next, it be repaid to the Treasurer on that day.

Committee meeting held at the Red Lion Inn, Nov. 2nd.

Ordered. That £66 be paid into the hands of Mr G. Fisher for the purpose of defraying the expenses of the election for the town of Cambridge.

At the general meeting of the Club, at the Red Lion Inn, Nov. 2nd, 1839, amendment of rules—

In place of Rule 16:

That the members of the Club shall dine together once annually in the Michaelmas term on a day to be appointed by the Committee: the Secretary giving to each member 10 days' notice of such dinner: and that members desirous of dining with the Club shall signify their intention of so doing to the Secretary not later than the third day before the dinner.

Committee meeting, Mr Stokes' rooms, Tuesday, Nov. 26th, 1839, to consider about the payment of Hunnybun's bill, and the share of each member for the dinner.

Share £1. 17s. 6d. Voted to be *too much*, being more than ten shillings above the usual price. And that Hunnybun be spoken to by the Treasurer on the subject, and reduce the charge.

(Later the whole charge was paid.)

At a Committee meeting held in Mr Savile's rooms on Saturday the 28th of Nov., it was resolved—

That a general meeting of the Club should be held at the Red Lion on Monday the 7th of December to take into consideration the propriety of establishing a Reading Room in connexion with the Club.

Resolved—

That a Ballot Box should be procured for the use of the Club.

At a general meeting of the Club held at the Red Lion Inn on Monday, Dec. 7th,

It was resolved—

That authority be given by the Club to a Committee to examine into the expediency of establishing a Reading Room and Smoking Room in connexion with the Club, and that they may be desired to present their report at the General Meeting next term.

At a Committee meeting held in Mr Lonsdale's rooms on Tuesday, 23rd February, 1841, It was determined by the Committee that a reading and smoking room should be established in connexion with the Club, and a sub-committee was formed for making arrangements for the same. They determined to engage rooms at Hutt's, Book-seller, Trinity St.

At a general meeting held at the Red Lion on Wednesday, Feb. 24th, 1841, the determination of the Committee about the reading rooms was read and put to the vote and was carried unanimously.

At a Committee meeting held in Mr Bentinck's rooms on Friday the 5th March, 1841, it was determined by the Committee that the reading and smoking rooms at Hutt's, Trin. St. should be opened on Monday the 8th inst.

In the Michaelmas Term 1840 the Treasurer had paid £48. 5s. 0d. of the subscriptions received into Barker's Bank five days before it suspended payment. This was lost; the rest of the subscriptions were paid into Messrs Mortlock's Bank at which the Club account (with the exception of an interlude during which it was at Messrs Fosters' Bank) has remained to the present day, though Mortlock's is now merged in Barclays Bank.

II. 1841–1843

U.P.C. ROOMS AT 29 TRINITY STREET

T H E Club entered upon a new stage of its history when on Monday, March 8th, 1841, it took possession of the rooms over the shop of Mr Richard Hutt, bookseller and stationer, at 29 Trinity Street. The rent appears to have been £90 a year for the furnished rooms. On the following day, at a Committee meeting held in the Club rooms, "the following laws were agreed upon for the regulation of the U.P.C. rooms".

1. That two rooms be provided for the use of the members of the "University Pitt Club".

2. That these rooms be opened from 10 o'clock a.m. till 10 p.m.

3. That no smoking be allowed in the lower Room under the penalty of £1.

4. That no cards be allowed in the Club Rooms under the penalty of £1.

5. That no Wine, Beer or Spirits be allowed in the Club Rooms under the penalty of £1.

6. That no property be removed from the Rooms under the penalty of 10s. per article.

7. That any member may introduce a friend, provided he be not resident in the University.

8. That it be the imperative duty of every officer of the U.P.C. to take notice of any infringement of the above rules.

Notwithstanding the cost of the preparation and use of the new rooms, the Club still continued to give active support to the Conservative cause. In May 1841, £50 was paid "in aid of the late Elections fund in Cambridge", and a sum of £100 to a Mr Fichtin, who may have been an election agent. In 1842 the Club paid £24. 5s. 0d. for meeting an account for newspapers incurred by the "Conservative Operatives Association". From this time onwards no further mention is made of political dinners attended by the whole Club. They may have continued as a matter of course, but the absence of any further reference to them seems rather to indicate that they had been discontinued.

The chief preoccupation, however, of the Club Committee in these years appears to have been the search for better rooms than those rented from Mr Hutt. A sub-committee of four was appointed in March 1842, by a Committee meeting held in Mr Archer Burton's rooms in Magdalene, to bring "definite plans" to the next full Committee. The sub-committee presented their report in April and recommended that the Club should build new rooms "on the premises of Dr Dyball in Bridge St." These premises, used later for billiard rooms, lay behind the house at 7 Bridge Street. This important project was duly debated in the rooms of Mr Bullock in Caius College. On the motion being put "That the Club do leave Hutt's for Dyball's", there voted five in favour and seven against.

The site, which the Club decided by this narrow majority not to occupy in 1842, was taken nearly seventy years later for the purposes of a motor garage by Messrs King and Harper.

It may be noted here that *Punch*[1] was first ordered for the Club rooms in October 1842, and its use has probably never been discontinued.

Hutt's rooms evidently gave dissatisfaction, for in spite of the rejection of the motion to build new rooms, notice to quit 29 Trinity Street was given in November 1842, and Mr G. A. F. Bentinck (Trinity), formerly President, Mr T. Robinson (Trinity), Treasurer, Mr T. L. French (Emmanuel), Secretary, were empowered to "treat with Metcalfe about his rooms". Mr Metcalfe had a furniture shop at 74 Bridge Street, at the south-east corner of All Saints' Passage, and the rooms in question were over this shop and approached from the Passage.

After receiving a report from this sub-committee it was unanimously resolved by a Committee held in Mr Blackburn's rooms in Trinity College to hire furnished rooms from Mr Metcalfe at an annual rent of £70, with a "composition" for firing and lighting the rooms which was settled later at £20 per annum.

It is formally recorded that the next meeting of the University Pitt Club "was held at their rooms in All Saints' Passage, February 8th, 1843".

[1] No. 1 of *Punch* was published in July 1841.

III. 1843–1866

U.P.C. ROOMS AT 74 BRIDGE STREET
(ALL SAINTS' PASSAGE)

THE removal to the new rooms at the corner of All Saints' Passage did not check the political interests of the Club. The Committee met in February 1843 in Lord Nelson's rooms in Trinity and agreed "that Members of the Committee endeavour to raise the sum of £100 by an extra subscription, to be set aside for the purposes of an election Fund".

It is no doubt to this Fund that the Prime Minister, Sir Robert Peel, referred in the following letter to his son, then in his third year at Trinity:

May 13, 1843.

My dear Frederick,

What are the facts of the case, as far as you are concerned, in respect to a subscription for the last election at Cambridge? I was told yesterday that a Club, I think the Pitt Club, had subscribed £100, that your name among others appeared in the subscription list, that a portion of the fund had been applied to bribery of voters, that the facts were known to the petitioners against the return, and will be brought before the Election Committee, which was appointed last night.

I feel very confident that if any improper use whatever has been made of the money it must have been altogether without your sanction or knowledge. But it may be as well that you should let me know what are the exact facts of the case, so far as you are concerned.

Did the subscribers to the fund employ any agent of their own or did they subscribe to some common fund?

Ever affectionately yours,

ROBERT PEEL.[1]

In 1901 Lord Nelson, then aged 78, wrote as follows from Trafalgar, Salisbury:

> I was President [of the Pitt Club] during the notable year of Fitzroy Kelly's Election, when I was summoned to appear before a Committee of the House of Commons with the Books of the Club. Happily they did without me and I was not called on to give evidence.

On March 22nd, at a Committee meeting held in the rooms of the U.P.C. and afterwards adjourned to Lord Nelson's rooms, it was unanimously agreed "that Mr Fitzroy Kelly be invited to meet the U.P.C. at dinner on Friday next", and with the same unanimity it was decided "that £60 be paid from the Election Fund into Mr Bartlett's hands towards the expenses of the Election".

The invitation from the Club was duly forwarded to Mr Kelly, but before he could accept it he had received a letter in the following terms from Dr W. Whewell, Master of Trinity and Vice-Chancellor of the University:

Trinity Lodge,
March 23rd, 1843.

Sir,

I have been informed that it is the intention of some members of the University to hold a dinner at a tavern with

---

[1] From *The Private Letters of Sir Robert Peel* (London, John Murray, 1920).

reference to your Election as Member of Parliament for this Borough. I beg you to allow me to state to you that I consider the attendance of persons of this University *In statu pupillari* at such a dinner would be highly objectionable and I hope you will do me the favour to give no encouragement to such an intention.

I am, Sir,

Your very obedient, humble Servant,

W. Whewell, V.C.

In consequence of this letter Mr Fitzroy Kelly wrote as follows to Mr S. T. Bartlett, who had been asked by the U.P.C. Committee to convey their invitation to him:

University Arms,

23rd March, 1843.

My dear Sir,

I had anticipated a high gratification in meeting my friends of the University Pitt Club to-morrow, but to-day I have received a letter from the Vice-Chancellor of which I enclose a copy.

I shall not trust myself to comment upon this letter. We must, however, make up our minds to submit to lawful authority. Pray tell your friends that this is a very severe disappointment to me but that I shall console myself with the hope of better times, and that I shall always retain a deep sense of obligation for the intended kindness.

I remain,

Very Faithfully yours,

Fitzroy Kelly.

There seems to be no reason for supposing that Dr Whewell's inhibition had reference to any questions of party politics. On becoming Vice-Chancellor in

1842 he had given special attention to problems of University discipline. In March 1843 his friend Archdeacon Hare had written to him to say that "from many reports which have reached me in the last six months, I am very much afraid that the additional burthen of the Vice-Chancellor's cares has somewhat ruffled you again, and called out the vehemence of the natural man, which it is always difficult to repress". Whewell replied to this friendly criticism in a letter of March 31st, 1843, in which he wrote:[1] "I have every reason to believe that those who have to do with me do not think me 'ruffled' and do not find me more vehement than what amounts to firmness. . . . I have things to do which some people will call oppressive offices; but only persons whom you would not agree with, any more than myself. I have tried to suppress pigeon-shooting in the outskirts of the town, uproar in the Senate House galleries, and dinners at taverns; and of course this makes detractors and railers." This letter was written only eight days, it will be seen, after his letter to Mr Fitzroy Kelly.

This excitement over, the political energy of the Club appears to have been exhausted, for only one more financial subvention of a political kind appears to have been made. This was in December 1843, when at a Committee meeting held in Mr W. S. Hodson's rooms in Trinity it was ordered "that £15 be paid to the Committee for promoting the

[1] Quoted from *The Life of William Whewell*, by Mrs Stair Douglas (Kegan Paul, Trench and Co., London, 1882), p. 287.

election of a Town Councillor for the West Barnwell Ward".

On April 28th, 1844, it was agreed "that letters put into the Pitt Letter Box be paid for from the Club money". This distinctive and almost unique privilege of membership has continued up to the present day.

At a Committee meeting at the Club rooms on November 1st, 1845, "It was resolved that Bradshaw's Railway Time Table should be taken in". It was in this year that the railway from London to Cambridge was constructed.

In 1847 a Club library was formed, "to contain all works of general interest and not merely novels". In December of that year the thanks of the Club were "presented to Mr Cox of Trin. Coll. for the handsome present of books to the Club library". Special subscriptions for the purchase of books for the library were made by many of the life members of the Club.

In 1848 a minute records that on March 1st it was resolved "that the present mode of lighting the Club by Gas be discontinued and that candles be used instead".

From 1849 until 1869 we have no further Minutes either of Committee or general meetings. The book for the entry of candidates' names, with the names of proposers and seconders and the dates of election, which came into use in March 1836, is preserved and this maintains a continuous record until April 1869. We also have the "Treasurer's Book" containing the terminal accounts from the Lent Term 1847 until

December 1867, when the removal of the Club from 74 Bridge Street to the new premises in Jesus Lane was in process of completion.

After 1843, there being apparently no further political activity, the Club rooms were given up to the purely private or social purposes of the members. The accounts for twenty years in the "Treasurer's Book" show recurrent payments in each term which give no indication of any activities except those of reading and writing within the Club rooms, or of any outside them. There are no records of dinners either for the Club in general or for the Committee. Candles, writing paper, periodicals and books are regular items in the accounts, with more occasional payments for furniture and repairs. In every term up to, but not after, 1852, a small charge appears "for mending pens". Presumably quills were then replaced by metal nibs. The rent paid to Metcalfe for the Club rooms over his furniture shop was £20 a quarter, during this period.

Mr Metcalfe had a clerk, Mr W. Todd, who received the payments from the Club. Mr Todd was alive in 1904 and gave the following details from memory: "The Club consisted of one large room with five windows as a reading and writing room and one small room for smoking. The rooms were let furnished. The members paid their subscriptions in Mr Metcalfe's office, and his clerk, Mr Todd, kept the accounts and rendered a statement to the Treasurer once a term. The Committee meetings were held in one of the Committee men's rooms, who gave a dinner and paid

31

for it. Each was supposed to give a dinner in his turn."

For the years 1852 and 1853 the accounts are in the neat handwriting of Mr C. Brinsley Marlay of Trinity College, who died in 1912 bequeathing to the University his art collection and a large endowment for its maintenance. His name is preserved in the Marlay extension of the Fitzwilliam Museum and the Marlay collection and curatorship there. Those for three years from May 1861 are in the no less neat handwriting of Leslie Stephen of Trinity Hall, first and greatest editor of the *Dictionary of National Biography*, who as the "Rev. L. Stephen" had been elected a member of the Club in the Lent Term 1860, after he had become Fellow and Assistant Tutor of his College and had taken Deacon's Orders. He rowed in his College boat for ten years, 1852–62, and helped to take it twice to the Headship, in 1859 and 1862. In 1864 most members of the Pitt Club went to Fenner's to see the celebrated match between Leslie Stephen, their Treasurer, and P. M. Thornton[1] of Jesus College. Stephen undertook to walk two miles before Thornton, starting with him, could run three. He started, as a College Tutor should, in respectable clothing, having discarded only coat and waistcoat. Presently he removed his collar. Soon his shirt became disorderly and embarrassed him, so he removed it altogether and cast it from him as he walked. He finished in trousers only, and boots; but Thornton caught him thirty yards from the tape among scenes of

[1] Later M.P. for Clapham.

32

great enthusiasm. It was in this year that Thornton, much assisted by Leslie Stephen's influence, successfully proposed to Oxford the institution of the Inter-University Athletic Sports.

The Pitt Club had become during those years what it has since remained, a purely social club.[1] Those who remembered it in the years just before 1867 said that while the increasing athleticism of the undergraduates both on land and water was well reflected inside the Club it never dominated it. The rowing men, especially of Third Trinity and Trinity Hall, were prominently represented in the Club. Members from St John's and other Colleges had relatively declined in numbers in comparison with those from Trinity, King's, Trinity Hall and Magdalene. The Trinity members were in a large majority because of the size of the College and the convenient proximity of the Club rooms.

In 1860 Dr Whewell, Master of Trinity, had already built the first of the College Courts named after him upon the site of the old Sun Hotel in Trinity Street, opposite the Trinity Great Gate. Before 1865 he had bought the land east of this first Court up to Sidney Street for the erection of his second Court. Building began in 1866, the year in which he died. It was completed and the rooms first occupied in October 1868.

We have seen that the Pitt Club rooms were over

[1] King Edward VII, then Prince of Wales, who came up to Trinity in 1861, was not allowed to join the Club because it was known as a political club. But it had no political activities then, and the last traces of political flavour must have died out soon after that date.

Mr Metcalfe's furniture shop, 74 Bridge Street, at the corner of All Saints' Passage. Mr Metcalfe as he prospered became a hunting man. He used to appear from his premises in pink coat and top boots upon hunting days. Perhaps he came to neglect his business; at all events Mr Bulstrode joined him in partnership in 1852 and bought him out in 1855. Mr Metcalfe retired to a small house in Green Street, while Mr Bulstrode became the landlord of the Club and received the rent of £80 per annum for the Club rooms.

Bulstrode's premises were included in Dr Whewell's purchase and the Pitt Club must have had notice to quit before 1866. The last quarter's rent paid by the Club was up to Christmas 1865. Very soon after that the premises must have been pulled down to make way for the eastern part of Whewell's second Court.

IV. 1866–1900

U.P.C. ROOMS IN JESUS LANE, BEFORE THEIR ENLARGEMENT

THUS dispossessed of the rooms they had used for twenty-three years, the members of the Club found that by a fortunate chance some premises that were much better suited to Club purposes than the rooms above Bulstrode's shop had become available. These were unexpectedly provided by the financial failure of some Turkish Baths that the "Roman Bath Company" had built upon the site of the Hoop Inn coach-yard, with an entrance from Jesus Lane.

The Hoop Inn in Bridge Street had been one of the chief coaching inns of Cambridge. William Wordsworth when he first arrived at Cambridge to join St John's College saw it, no doubt with much relief, as he descended from the coach to stretch his long legs. He has preserved its memory for ever by his reference to it in the *Prelude*: "And at the *Hoop* alighted, famous Inn".

The beautiful early eighteenth-century brickwork of the front of the Inn may still be seen in Bridge Street above the ground floor now debased by garage entrances and shop fronts. The coach-yard behind it had formerly an archway approach from Bridge Street and extended eastward behind the houses in Jesus Lane to reach Park Street. The assembly room of the Inn was at the Park Street end and is now the theatre of the A.D.C. The coach-yard had also a wide gateway to Jesus Lane through the gap now filled by the Pitt Club portico and entrances.

As coaching declined, so did the Hoop Inn. In 1853 all the "Hoop estate" was conveyed to William Ekin, a brewer, except the body of the Inn itself in Bridge Street, which remained as a small hotel with a licensed bar until 1910. Most of the coach-yard and its approach from Jesus Lane, but without the assembly room in Park Street, was sold by Mr Ekin to the "Roman Bath Company" for £2077.

The classical portico now to be seen in Jesus Lane gave entrance to the Bath. The present reading room of the Pitt Club with its roof supported by Doric columns was constructed to contain a plunge bath and to serve as a cooling room for those who had been through the heating processes in other rooms beyond it. The "Roman Bath" was really a Turkish Bath: it appears to have been a complete and early failure. In October 1865, Mr Chappell, mortgagee of the Bath Company, sold the property for £2700 to Sir Matthew Digby Wyatt,[1] a member of the family that produced so many architects. He had been Secretary to the Executive Committee of the Great Exhibition of 1851 and had designed among many other buildings those of Paddington Station and (with Gilbert Scott) the

[1] Born 1820, died 1877. In 1869 he was appointed the first Slade Professor of Fine Art in Cambridge.

India Office in London, and Addenbrooke's Hospital in Cambridge. It may be surmised that we owe the architecture of the former Roman Bath and present Pitt Club portico and pillared room, not unpleasing in design, to him, or, if not to him, to his elder brother Thomas Henry Wyatt. It was the latter who designed the Assize Courts at Cambridge that reflect a similarly timid use of a classical style. It may also be guessed that Sir Digby Wyatt's purchase of the property was in some way connected with non-payment by the Company of his professional fees. At all events he very soon, probably early in 1866, leased one part of the Roman Bath premises to the University Pitt Club and a rather smaller part for use as public billiard rooms. The exact date of this first lease to the Club is not known, because the lease was surrendered upon its renewal in 1887 on different terms. The partition of the site between the Club and the billiard rooms is shown in Plans I a and II a. The rent paid by the Club was £49. 3s. 4d. ("rent less income tax") half-yearly, and the first instalment was paid in October 1866.

The Pitt Club was preparing in 1865 to move to its new quarters. A list of special subscriptions "towards furnishing the New Rooms" is preserved and £210 was paid into the bank as a result before the end of November 1865. In March 1866, payment of £50 is made "on account" to Bulstrode the furniture dealer, no doubt in respect of furniture and fittings for the new rooms. The "Treasurer's Book" closes in December 1867, with a credit due to the Club of £163. 13s. 2½d.

after various disbursements, probably chiefly for furnishing. A "new Monogram Die" had been provided also for the Club notepaper.

A Mrs Purchas appears to have been engaged as housekeeper in the new Club rooms. Payments to her begin in March 1866.

We may suppose that when the Michaelmas Term of 1866 began, the Club was comfortably established in its new home. It has been noted already that no minutes of Committee or other meetings have been preserved for the years between 1848 and 1869. From 1869 onwards we have full records of all the Club's proceedings. The gap in the records is well bridged, as we have seen, by the continuity of the accounts and of the membership list, and the removal to Jesus Lane probably made little significant difference to the life and practices of the Club. We find that by 1869 the custom of having a young "don" as President was established. The Committee for that year consisted of the President, Mr R. C. Jebb[1] of Trinity, the Treasurer, Mr Walter Durnford[2] of King's, the Secretary, C. E. Oldman of Trinity, with seven other members. It is clear that the government of the Club had fallen into the hands of the Committee, subject to the powers of a general meeting rarely exercised, and that the election of new members was a function reserved for the

[1] Later Sir Richard Claverhouse Jebb, O.M., Litt.D.; Regius Professor of Greek and M.P. for the University; born 1841, died 1905.

[2] Later Sir Walter Durnford, G.B.E.; Fellow of Eton and Provost of King's; temporary President 1919; died 1926.

R. C. Jebb, M.A., *Trinity*   A. C. D. Ryder, *St John's*
PRESIDENT

J. Blake-Humphrey, *Trinity*   C. Pitt-Taylor, *Trinity*
SECRETARY

W. Durnford, *King's*
TREASURER

F. Hunt, *Trinity*
LIBRARIAN

U.P.C. COMMITTEE, 1868

Committee. Dinners for the whole Club had probably been discontinued a quarter of a century earlier, but the Committee meetings were held commonly after a dinner given by one or more of the members.

After a Committee meeting in Mr G. E. Welby's rooms in Trinity on June 7th, 1871, the Secretary, Mr E. S. L. Randolph of Trinity, makes the following note: "It might be suggested that the disuse of the ancient loyal toasts is wholly contrary to the wishes and feelings of our predecessors, and we go a step further therefore and propose that they should be revived on the next and earliest opportunity." At the two next Committee meetings, toasts of the Queen and Royal Family and of the Immortal Memory of Mr Pitt were "revived". At a Committee dinner given by the Hon. A. T. Lyttelton[1] "the usual toasts were drunk". Finally, at a dinner given to the Committee by Mr Jebb, the toasts were "The Queen", "The Pious and Immortal Memory of William Pitt" and "Our next merry meeting". These three toasts, the second of course to be drunk in silence, have ever since been honoured at subsequent Committee dinners. Any occasional toast proposed is drunk between the second and third of these.

At a general meeting on May 12th, 1870, it was proposed from the Chair by Mr Jebb, and seconded by Mr Walter Durnford, "That a boat be sent to Henley Regatta to row under the name of the Pitt Boat". This

[1] Later first Master of Selwyn (1882–93) and Bishop of Southampton (1898–1903); died 1903.

was carried unanimously, and £50 was voted by the Club to defray the expenses of the crew. The following crew entered for the Grand Challenge Cup at Henley, where they lodged with a Third Trinity Four entered for the Wyfold Challenge Cup:

		st.	lb.
Bow	W. M. Browne	10	9
2	R. I. Blackburne	11	2
3	A. J. G. Watkin	12	4
4	J. A. Campbell	11	2
5	J. F. Strachan	12	3
6	J. H. Ridley	11	12
7	E. S. L. Randolph	11	$6\frac{1}{2}$
St.	J. H. D. Goldie	12	6
Cox	A. V. Pinckney		

In the first heat, Kingston R.C. beat the Pitt boat by one length in 7 mins. 32 secs., the Pitt having the admittedly worse station on the old Henley course; in the second, London R.C. beat Eton College by $\frac{2}{3}$rd length in 7 mins. $36\frac{1}{2}$ secs.; in the final the Oxford Etonians beat London R.C. by one length in 7 mins. $17\frac{4}{5}$ secs.

This experiment has not since been repeated by the Club.

In 1871 new apartments were completed for Mrs Purchas the housekeeper. These were made on the first floor above the hall and part of the reading room.

In 1873 the Secretary, Mr Hugh Neville of Magdalene, records that "at the commencement of the May Term the Pitt Boy broke out into buttons and a tall hat with a silver cord round it; this of course will be an important date in the annals of the Cambridge University Pitt Club."

In October 1873 Mr Purchas was appointed Steward of the Club.

In March 1874 a Committee was held to consider a complaint made by the Rev. E. H. Morgan, Pro-proctor, "that the waiter of the Club had rudely told him on Sunday afternoon that no Proctors were admitted to the Club by the order of the Committee, and that the Club was used as a sanctuary by capless and gownless undergraduates". Mr A. A. Tilley[1] of King's, Secretary, forwarded a suitable apology to the Proctors, and the minutes record that "The 'waiter' received a severe reprimand for his audacious conduct and was warned that another fiction on his part would ensure his immediate dismissal".

The truth as narrated long after by Mr Sydney Holland of Trinity Hall, later the 2nd Viscount Knutsford and then an undergraduate member of the Club, was that Mr Morgan of Jesus, known as "Red Morgan" to distinguish him from "Black Morgan" who later became Master of Jesus, was a man of stalwart carriage and fierce countenance. He had noticed an undergraduate wearing no gown on Sunday, who took refuge from him in the Pitt Club. "Red Morgan" attempted to follow him into the Club. The tiny page-boy, recently glorified by top hat and buttons, confronted the Proctor and his bull-dogs, all in full Sunday costume, upon the steps, held out his arm and said, "No Proctors allowed in 'ere, Sir." "Who says so?" asked Morgan. "The Committee says so, Sir." With

---

[1] Fellow of King's; oldest resident member (1935).

that Mr Morgan withdrew his forces and wrote his letter. The Club were not seriously displeased with their "waiter", but happily this was the last occasion of any conflict with the proctorial body.[1]

In February 1876 Mr Jebb resigned the presidency of the Club upon leaving Cambridge to take up his duties as Professor of Greek in Glasgow University. The Committee wrote to express the indebtedness of the Club for his long services and elected Mr Joseph Prior, M.A., Fellow and Tutor of Trinity College, to succeed him. It was the success of Jebb as President that ensured the maintenance of the practice already established of electing a resident Fellow, young enough to keep in touch with undergraduate life, to preside over the Club and to maintain its best interests. Jebb's feeling for the Club is well shown in a private letter written in 1873 to his future wife, then in the United States:

Tonight I am going to dine with the Committee of my dearly loved Pitt Club.... Our host this evening is a very nice Eton boy who has just come up to Trinity, Lord Stopford. It is so pleasant now and then to have an opportunity of seeing in this way some of the best undergraduates, not as a "don", but as the head of one of their own Societies.[2]

[1] At least until 1930, when a Proctor complained to the President of an undergraduate having escaped from him into the Club. Later, in 1933, the Committee and the proctorial body entered into a kind of "non-aggression pact" by which the Committee agreed to take action against "any member whose conduct in the Club had later given rise to a breach of University discipline". So far no such occasion has arisen.

[2] *Life and Letters of Sir Richard Jebb, O.M., Litt.D.* (Camb. Univ. Press, 1907), p. 148.

In May 1877 Mr C. J. White was appointed Steward of the Club to succeed Mr Purchas.

In October 1878 the Secretary, the Hon. A. G. Lawley, brought before the Committee when dining with the Hon Alfred Lyttelton and Mr E. O. P. Bouverie a letter from Vincent's Club, Oxford, offering honorary membership of that Club to any members of the Pitt Club visiting Oxford. The invitation was accepted and reciprocal privileges were accorded to Vincent's Club. This resolution was incorporated in the rules at a Committee meeting in March 1884.

In February 1881 the Secretary, the Hon. J. ff. Wallop, wrote to the agent acting for Lady Wyatt, widow of Sir Digby Wyatt, to ask whether the Club might in 1886, on the termination of their lease, extend their premises by taking in those adjoining the Club, at that time in the hands of the proprietor of the billiard rooms (which had been unwarrantably called the "Pitt Billiard Rooms"). He was informed that no proposals for extension of the Club premises could then be entertained. In May of the same year a proposal was put forward to enlarge the smoking room, and a scheme for doing so was approved by the committee and executed in the winter vacation. It was not, however, completed before the beginning of the Lent Term. It was suggested that members coming up early should be accommodated by half the Club being screened off from the scene of the alterations, but this inconvenient arrangement was made unnecessary by the hospitality of the A.D.C., who admitted members of the Club to temporary membership.

In May 1883 Mr Prior resigned the office of President and the Rev. F. Gunton, M.A., of Magdalene College, was appointed to succeed him.

At the beginning of the following Michaelmas Term the Secretary, Mr J. E. K. Studd,[1] wrote on behalf of the Club to invite H.R.H. Prince Edward of Wales,[2] a Freshman at Trinity College, to accept membership of the Club, and to offer honorary membership to his tutor, the Rev. J. N. Dalton. Both invitations were accepted.

In the Easter Term of 1887 Mr Gunton resigned, and Mr Montague Rhodes James, Fellow of King's College,[3] was elected President.

In May 1888 it was decided that a telephone should be taken (the first telephone exchange having been opened in London in 1879). In 1890 the weighing machine, on which members may still weigh themselves with some approximation to accuracy, was purchased.

Two problems engaged the Committee's attention in the next year or two. The first concerned the library. In March 1891, "It was suggested that, with a view to putting a stop to the almost wholesale abstraction of Library books, one bookcase should be fortified with

[1] Lord Mayor of London 1928–9.

[2] Later the Duke of Clarence; died 1892.

[3] Later Provost of King's, Provost of Eton, O.M., Litt.D., D.D.

doors, lock, and key; that in this case all the best books and standard works should be kept, the key to be in the possession of Mr White." This suggestion was confirmed in the following October, but the scheme did not entirely cure the evil, for the Steward at the end of every term still had to send a handcart round to certain lodging-houses in the proximity of the Club to collect Club library books. Indeed, it was said with some accuracy that the Pitt Club library at that time formed the foundation of a large number of country house libraries in England.

The Committee encountered their second problem when they wished to reverse the existing regulation which allowed smoking in the reading room (now the library) but not in the main sitting room. But a sparsely attended general meeting in December 1893 passed a resolution against their wishes, to permit smoking in both rooms. The Committee were not satisfied, and sent out a circular restating their original proposal, and urging their belief "that promiscuous smoking would be prejudicial to the best interests of the Club": they further invited any dissentients to call another general meeting to reconsider the issue. Their prompt if unconstitutional challenge was not taken up, and the reading room, no longer to be sullied by the fumes of tobacco, was more comfortably furnished and honoured with the introduction of a carpet.

In February 1893 the Committee "unanimously resolved to fit up the Club with the electric light at an estimated cost of about £40".

In May 1899 Dr James expressed his desire to resign the presidency and suggested W. M. Fletcher,[1] Fellow of Trinity, as his successor. On May 15th Dr James gave a farewell dinner to the Committee at which he introduced Mr Fletcher, and on October 28th, the presidency was transferred.

[1] Later Sir W. M. Fletcher, K.B.E., F.R.S.; First Secretary of the Medical Research Council; died 1933.

V. 1900–1914

THE DEVELOPMENT OF THE CLUB ROOMS IN JESUS LANE

IN January 1900 alterations to the Club were discussed. They were finally approved in January 1901 after the plans had been exhibited in the Club Room for members' approval. They were not of a far-reaching scale, and were chiefly devoted to obtaining more light for the large room.

Mr C. J. White, who had been Steward of the Club for twenty-three years, retired in 1900. The Committee decided to give him a pension of £75 per annum for life, and F. Rees was appointed in his place.

In May 1901 Lord Howick,[1] who was then Secretary, suggested that there should be a Pitt Club Lawn near Grassy Corner for spectators of the May Races. The suggestion was followed up and the Pitt Lawn became an immensely popular resort for members and their May Week guests.

At the same Committee meeting the President announced that he had persuaded their landlord, Mr Wyatt, not only to give the Committee a further 40 years' lease of their existing premises, but also to transfer to them for the same period the lease of the rest of the site of the former "Roman Bath Company",

---

[1] Now the Fifth Earl Grey.

47

which included the billiard rooms next door and two bedrooms upstairs formerly leased to the Hoop Hotel (see Plans I*a* and II*a*). Thus the way was cleared for the rapid development of the Club buildings which took place during the following ten years.

The first step in this development was the provision of a dining room on the first floor of the billiard room premises, approached by a staircase from the entrance hall. This met a very urgent need, for until October 1901 the only luncheon that a member could get in the Club was a plate of sandwiches or cold beef, and a glass of beer, which had to be consumed in the main Club sitting room. The necessary alterations were carried out in the Long Vacation of 1901; at the same time a kitchen was established in the basement, and the lavatories were moved downstairs, the wash-basins alone being retained on the ground floor. Mr E. H. Parker,[1] who had succeeded Mr H. A. Arkwright[2] as Treasurer in 1899, had £1400 in hand which had been expected to be ample to pay for the alterations. But during the work in the basement "the Club's drainage system, long and fondly believed to be adequate, was found to be worthless where it was found at all", and it had to be renewed entirely. The result was a final deficit of nearly £300. To meet this a general meeting held on May 11th, 1902, adopted the suggestion of the Committee that the entrance fee should be raised by half

[1] King's College, Hon. LL.D. 1922; Director Barclays Bank; d. 1928.

[2] Magdalen College, Oxford; O.U.C.C. 1895; Local Director Barclays Bank, Cambridge 1898–9.

a guinea and that an appeal for special subscriptions should be made to present members. This appeal raised over £200.

At the meeting of the Committee on January 30th, 1902, "The secretary, in the name of the members of the U.P.C., asked the President to accept a silver bowl as an expression of the Club's gratitude to him for his exertions in the alterations which had lately taken place in the Club premises."

In January 1904 F. Rees resigned his post as Steward and D. G. Marshall, who was then in the employment of the Trinity College kitchens, was appointed in his place. Mr Marshall's services to the Club were very remarkable. It was he who instituted a system of catering on an elaborate scale, supplying meals, not only to the Club, but also to undergraduates living in lodgings, so that during his tenure of the Stewardship the Club acquired a large and elaborate kitchen plant and profited very considerably by sales of food and wine. Until he came into office, the dining room account showed a regular terminal deficit, but after one term of his management a profit of £120 appeared. Again, the first of the long series of Pitt Club balls was instituted in 1905. For the first two balls the catering was done externally and a considerable financial loss was incurred; the third, however, was under Mr Marshall's management and a profit was made which more than covered the previous loss. Later, he conceived and carried out the ingenious scheme of growing mushrooms under the arches of what is now the main Club dining room.

Finally, the "Napoleon of the Pitt", as he came to be called, laid the foundations of his present prosperous garage and aerodrome business by providing two private cars which members might hire. One of these, with its smart chauffeur, was regularly to be seen waiting outside the Club in Jesus Lane.

In the Long Vacation of 1904, some improvements in the decoration and lighting of the main sitting room were carried out, for which Mr Gaselee, then a member of the Committee, chose a clock. At the meeting of the Committee in December 1904 the clock was "commented on as being unsuitable to the room in style, unable to keep time, and not sufficiently clear in the face, however the Committee decided to put up with it as a whimsy of the aforesaid member".[1] At the same meeting the minutes record that: "Mr Gaselee sang a song in a foreign tongue immediately after dinner".

It has already been recorded on p. 14 that Mr F. C. Simpson presented an original button of the Pitt uniform to the Club in 1904. The button bears behind it the name of the makers, Firmin and Sons. It was found that this firm in St Martin's Lane, London, still had the die for the buttons in their possession, and an order for new buttons was promptly executed by the firm, although the die had been unused and forgotten for well over half a century. At first it was proposed that the wearing of these buttons should be restricted to

[1] It was "put up with" until the Long Vacation 1933, when the smoking room was refurnished, and a wall clock was bought to replace it.

members of the Committee. But this occasioned such a storm of protest that the Committee had to give way and to allow all members of the Club to wear the buttons.

The Minutes from April 1905 to May 1906 are in the handwriting of the Hon. G. W. Lyttelton and contain many entertaining passages. At the meeting when it was decided that no member of the Club should at any time owe more than £20 to the dining room, he records that only four members of the Committee were present, "the other members, with a self-effacement which is all too rare, failing to put in an appearance". At a meeting in November 1905 there was a "long but indecisive discussion as to the best method of celebrating the centenary of the birth and death of Mr Pitt (which events *both* took place on Jan. 23, 1806)". The following February the library was recatalogued, and "it was decided that the back numbers of *The Times* and the *Illustrated London News*, which for fifty years past have been incased at the Club's expense in tasteful and costly binding, should be sold as soon as possible to any person or institution who might be simple enough to buy them." Eventually all the surplus periodicals and books, except the *Illustrated London News* and *Punch*, were sold to Deighton and Bell for £65. 0s. 0d. It was also during the secretaryship of Lyttelton that a member overstepped the limit of his skill in spelling in suggesting "that soup be optional with sweat at Luncheon". The solemn reply was that "the Committee are unable to believe that such a dish could ever be generally popular in the Club".

Negotiations for the purchase of the freehold of the Club and billiard room premises, for which the Committee had been given a 40 years' lease in 1901, were opened in November 1906, and on December 4th the President announced that they had resulted in a definite offer. Mr Wyatt, the owner, was willing to sell the property to the Club for £5975. 0s. 0d., this sum being that which would purchase sufficient India $3\frac{1}{2}\%$ stock to produce as interest the amount that the Club had formerly been paying as rent, namely £196. 9s. 6d.

The Committee were unanimously in favour of accepting this offer, but considered that a matter which would have such a profound effect on the future of the Club ought to be submitted to a general meeting. The meeting was held on December 6th, and the proposals of the Committee were unanimously approved, but as the attendance was small it was decided to hold a further meeting in the following January, and meanwhile to send a circular to all past and present members of the Club stating the means by which the Committee intended to meet the situation.

The circular, sent out over the President's signature, gave a short account of the history of the Club buildings, pointing out how the part of the premises of the original "Roman Bath" assigned to the Club suffered from "the intricacy with which they interdigitated in both horizontal and vertical planes with the part leased as public Billiard rooms to another tenant", and describing how the Club had come to obtain a lease of the whole premises in 1901 which enabled them to establish the dining room; it then announced the offer, which had been accepted, for the purchase of the freehold. It continued: "The Committee are faced with the task of finding the purchase money. Very fortunately indeed they find themselves able to leave £3500 of the whole amount on Mortgage at $3\frac{1}{2}\%$. Of the rest the Club can afford to pay £1000 to £1200 and are able to raise the balance from their bankers upon a personal guarantee." Finally the circular pointed out that, though the purchase would inevitably postpone further improvements in the Club rooms which had long been needed and, indeed, claimed by members, yet "the Committee could not be justified in expending further sums in the improvement of premises held only upon lease: the purchase of the freehold is properly a necessary condition for the very improvement which it delays".

On January 26th, 1907, the general meeting was duly held and the Committee were empowered to proceed with the purchase. This they did, and further appointed Dr M. R. James, Mr Owen Hugh Smith, Mr W. M. Fletcher, Mr E. M. Clark, Mr W. Dudley Ward, Mr Lionel de Rothschild and the Hon. G. W. Lyttelton as Trustees to hold the property on behalf of the Club.

Two days before this general meeting, in the early morning of January 24th, 1907, a fire broke out, which entirely destroyed the Club dining room, the Steward's room and offices, with a great part of the staircase. Little damage was done to the rest of the Club except by the water from the fire hoses pouring down from the roof. All the Club records and papers were saved, but many of the portraits of distinguished old members which had been collected by the President, and which had hung on the walls of the dining room and of the staircase, were destroyed.

The outbreak of fire was noticed shortly after 3 o'clock in the morning by the three policemen on duty in Sidney Street, and the alarm was at once given to the Central Fire Station, but not before the dining room was already well alight. The Town Council had recently bought a new fire engine, and this was its baptism of fire. *The Cambridge Chronicle* of January 25th records: "The Council's new investment proved the value of steam pressure in cases of emergency. . . . For over two hours a pressure of about 90 lbs. to the square inch was maintained and a large supply of water drawn from a source[1] which experience has proved to be invariably adequate. By about a quarter to six the fire was practically stamped out."

The fire was probably caused by a well grate in the dining room. The weather at the time being very severe, the fire was kept red hot all the evening. When the Steward left shortly before 11 o'clock there was no

---

[1] This source was a fire hydrant in Jesus Lane. When the fire brigade arrived they found the cover of this hydrant frozen fast, and were unable to open it. The situation had become serious when it was suddenly relieved by the appearance of Mr Beattie, the hairdresser, with a kettle of boiling water. It appeared that it was his invariable, and on this occasion most fortunate, habit to "pop the kettle on" whenever he got up in the morning, even when forcibly awaked at 5 a.m.

sign of danger, but no doubt the floor below the grate had already been affected, and must have burst into flames soon after his departure.

Next morning Marshall grappled with the situation with his usual promptness and efficiency. He set the staff to work to clear the water out of the kitchen, which was two feet in depth, and breakfasts were dispatched as usual to the members who were accustomed to have a substantial breakfast sent to their lodgings from the Pitt kitchen on a hunting morning. By Saturday the 26th, the Club was reopened, and meals were served as usual in the Club Library, which he had turned into a temporary dining room, and it was thus unnecessary to take advantage of the offers of hospitality which were received from the Hawks Club, the A.D.C. and the Conservative Club.

The fire left the Committee in a gravely embarrassing position. The loss of furniture, pictures, and dining room equipment was fully covered by the insurance, but the rebuilding of the dining room and staircase, and the reinstatement of the Club's billiard room tenants, whose premises had suffered considerable damage, would have involved them in a debt of £1800 to add to the debt of £4800 which was already owing on the recent purchase of the freehold. Further, the incorporation of the billiard rooms was essential for any permanent improvement in the Club buildings. This would involve paying Messrs Orme, their tenants, for the surrender of their lease which had five more years to run, thus increasing the Club's debt; but to have rebuilt the Club without incorporating the rooms would have been a most improvident policy.

The improvement most urgently demanded by members was the provision of a more suitable kitchen. The one then in use was in the basement and immediately underneath the main Club sitting room. It was small and badly ventilated, and the increasingly popular luncheons and dinners which Marshall provided demanded a larger room for their preparation. What is more, every evening between 7 and 8 o'clock the Club sitting room was filled with a grey and oily haze which oozed up through the floor from the subterranean kitchen. The obvious escape from this situation was to move the kitchen into one billiard room, and to use the second and larger one as the Club dining room.

After long consideration the Committee eventually decided that it would be wiser, and ultimately cheaper, to take the bolder course, namely, to obtain possession at once of the adjoining premises, and to postpone the question of the reconstruction of the first floor except for rebuilding the outside walls and placing a roof over them. Negotiations were consequently opened with Messrs Orme, who agreed to surrender the remainder of their lease in return for a payment of £250.

An appeal was sent out to past and present members to assist the Club in this crisis, which brought in above £1000. This generous assistance enabled the Committee to carry out a programme of complete restoration in addition to the alterations which they had already decided to make. The changes which were actually made in the Long Vacation of 1907 can be seen in Plans I*b* and II*b*. They were:

1. The conversion of one billiard room into a dining room and the other into a kitchen.

2. The straightening of the wall between the entrance hall and what now became the kitchen passage.

3. The rebuilding of the main staircase and the first floor.

4. The construction of a passage across the roof of the new kitchen to a room hitherto leased to the Hoop Hotel, of which possession was now taken.

At the meeting of the Committee in the following October Mr E. M. Clark, the Treasurer, reported that he had purchased a cottage in Sabberton's yard adjoining the Club on his own responsibility. The Treasurer's action was gratefully confirmed and three years later the cottage was incorporated into the Club, the ground floor being turned into a serving room for the main dining room, and the first floor into a serving room for the Hoop Room. At the same meeting Mr Gaselee was thanked for having "generously presented the Club with a bust of Mr Pitt". This bust now stands in a special niche built for it when the dining room was panelled in 1927.

The room which had formerly been leased to the Hoop Hotel was converted into a private dining room. It naturally came to be called "The Hoop Room", and in 1911 it was formally decided by the Committee that "The Private dining room should continue to be called the Hoop Room to commemorate the relation of the Club's room to the former Hoop Hotel premises, the Hoop Hotel having last year been abandoned and converted into shops and offices". It was first used for dining by the Committee on October 24th, 1907, and the Minutes record that it was found eminently satisfactory for that purpose.

Some members of the Committee considered that the establishment of the private dining room was an occasion for a relaxation in the Club rule, which states that "No Member shall introduce Ladies into any part of the Club premises". The question was settled at a Committee meeting in November 1907 when the Minutes record that "With regard to the much debated question as to whether members of the fair sex should be allowed to dine with Members of the Club in the Private Dining Room, Mr Durnford[1] with great vehemence proposed the motion 'That Ladies shall on no account be allowed to enter the Dining Room'. Mr Powell[2] seconded the proposal, which was carried by the smallest majority possible".

Another change also resulted from the existence of the private dining room. The custom of the Committee had been to dine together at least once a term, two members acting as hosts on each occasion. Before October 1907 these dinners took place in the rooms of one of the two hosts and, according to another custom,

[1] R. S. Durnford. Later a master at Eton. Killed in the Great War.

[2] E. W. Powell. Later a master at Eton. Killed in the Alps in 1933.

the London evening papers were always sent round with the Ballot Box from the Club to the rooms where the dinner was to be held. But after this date Committee dinners were usually given in the Hoop Room, though the occasional dinners given by the President and Treasurer were still held in the former's rooms in College or in their respective private houses.

The President viewed this change with disfavour, and at the farewell dinner which he gave in his rooms in Trinity, he "urged that the old practice of dining in each other's rooms should be introduced again. The present practice has the advantage of ensuring an admirable and well-served dinner; but it is open to criticism in that all the dinners resemble each other, while the two hosts have no functions at all save to pay for the dinner." In the discussion that followed Dr Fletcher's suggestion, most of the Committee favoured a reversion to the old practice. Nothing definite was decided, though there was a strong feeling that "it would be pleasant to revive the former system except in those cases where circumstances were adverse".[1]

[1] The pre-war Committees of course always devoted themselves primarily to the business of the Club at their meetings, but when the business had been efficiently dispatched, they usually employed the remainder of the evening with games or trials of skill, at which their enjoyment, if not their proficiency, was well ensured by the excellence of the dinner supplied by their hosts. For example on April 21st, 1913, at a meeting from which the President "much to his and the Committee's regret" was perforce absent, "the Hon. Sec. was heard to state that he wished the President was present to compete at push halfpenny with him"; again, on January 26th, 1914, at the end of the meeting, "The Committee divided into pairs, and competed in a game of

In spite of the feelings of this Committee, post-war Committees eventually found it more convenient and economical to dine in the Hoop Room, and to share the expense of the dinner amongst themselves. The President and Treasurer, however, continued to invite the Committee to dinner once a year.

After 1908 the Club entered upon a period of comparatively uneventful prosperity. The Minutes record little but the regular elections and decisions to refurnish wholly or in part one or other of the Club rooms. In January 1910 they decided that "when the Committee meet at dinner either tail coats or dinner jackets may be worn". In the same year the Hoop Room was panelled, the architect being Mr Henry Martineau Fletcher. The old dining room on the first floor was also redecorated and refurnished. Later the Committee agreed that it "should be used only by members of the Club and that silence should be enjoined on all using it until the hour of 8 p.m.".

One further purchase was made when in December 1912 the Committee gave £340 for three cottages commonly known as the Wallis Cottages. They lay at the back of No. 10 Jesus Lane, and were built against the A.D.C. Theatre. They were subsequently pulled down, and after the War the site was made rectangular in shape by an exchange of land with the Club's

---

skill which involved the use of a table, two Tennis balls, a good deal of coolness, and half-a-crown. All went well until Mr Davies, in the heat of the contest, upset a large tray of drinks, after which the Committee retired to bed."

neighbour, the Society of Friends, and the windows in the main Club sitting room were opened on to it.

Several domestic problems occupied the attention of the Committee in the years immediately preceding the War. In the October Term 1911 an Advisory Board was created of four resident life members to make recommendations on graduate candidates for election to the Club, as it had been found that the ordinary Committee was not sufficiently well acquainted with their characteristics to decide whether they would be suitable members of the Club or not. In the same term a further change was made in the rule concerning the election of Freshmen. Up till 1901 Freshmen could be elected immediately on their arrival in Cambridge. At that date it was thought better that they should not be eligible for election during their first term, but now a compromise was reached by which they could be elected after the division of their first term. This revision was ratified by a general meeting.

It was also during the October Term of 1911 that the Club servants were put into a livery of a similar design to that which was believed to have been in use in the household of William Pitt.

In the May Term 1912 the Committee determined upon a restriction of postage facilities for graduate members, as it was found that some of them were conducting their whole correspondence from the Club room. Later the restriction was incorporated in the rule which does not allow resident or local graduate members to avail themselves of the privilege of having their letters stamped free for them in the Club.

The increasing prosperity of the Club may be judged from the fact that at Christmas 1909 £700 had been paid to Mr Wyatt in reduction of the mortgage of £3500. At the end of 1911 a further £1000 was paid, and by Michaelmas 1914 the whole sum had been paid. Naturally this paying off of the mortgage made impossible the expenditure of money on badly needed improvements. Members of to-day who have the use of the extraordinarily well-appointed Club rooms, unrivalled at either University, have much for which to thank their predecessors, who suffered from many inconveniences in order that the debt on the purchase of the freehold, which gave the Club its security of position, might be paid off as soon as possible.

On May 4th, 1914, the resignation of Dr Fletcher was announced to the Committee as he was due to leave Cambridge to take up Government work in London. Mr Gaselee was proposed as his successor and was elected President at the general meeting on May 11th. At a Committee meeting on June 3rd the Secretary, Geoffrey Hopley,[1] entered in the Minute Book the following minute describing Dr Fletcher's services to the Club:

It is perhaps not out of place to summarize very shortly some of the services Dr Fletcher rendered to the Club. It is almost entirely owing to him that the Club kitchens and

[1] Joined the Grenadier Guards at the outbreak of war and died of wounds May 12th, 1915.

dining-room are now in so satisfactory a state. Before he became President it was impossible to get a proper meal on the Club premises. He did all that was possible to improve matters in this respect, but was hampered by the limited space at his disposal. Then, as a blessing in disguise, came the fire in January 1907 and, like another Christopher Wren, Dr Fletcher made the most of his chance. He was largely responsible for the appeal for money to past members of the Club, and with the money so obtained he was enabled to improve and add to the Club premises. The present dining-room was brought into use, and since then the success of the kitchens has been assured.

At the same time, Dr Fletcher was setting on foot the scheme for the purchase of the Freehold, which is now on the verge of being satisfactorily completed, and the importance of which can hardly be over-estimated. Dr Fletcher has also done an immense amount to improve the appearance and comfort of the Club—notably in collecting the prints which are so much appreciated by all members.

In recognition of all these services, the Committee, in combination with past members of the Committee who had served under Dr Fletcher, presented him with a clock.[1]

---

[1] For the clock Mr Gaselee devised the following inscription:

HOC HOROLOGIUM

WALTERO MORLEY FLETCHER

SODALICII

IN PIAM ET IMMORTALEM MEMORIAM
WILLELMI PITT

APUD CANTABRIGIENSES INCOHATI

PRAESIDI

PER XV ANNOS RE FELICISSIME ADMINISTRATA

D. D.

SODALES COLLEGAE AMICI

A.S. MDCCCCXIIII.

VI. 1914–1935

THE PITT CLUB DURING AND
AFTER THE WAR

W A R conditions naturally brought great changes to the Club. At the beginning of the October Term 1914 all the existing Committee had joined the forces. To fill their places a provisional committee was elected by the President and Treasurer, and Mr R. R. Sedgwick consented to act as temporary Secretary (an office which in fact he held till the end of 1917). The Club continued in a tenuous existence as more and more men left Cambridge for the front. Officers of the Cambridgeshire battalion of the Suffolk Regiment, and of the Cambridge Territorials, which were stationed in Cambridge, were made honorary members in 1914; and in 1915 a temporary rule was made allowing members to introduce to the Club any number of officers on active service quartered in Cambridge. Nevertheless the membership dwindled steadily, and it was found increasingly difficult to keep the Club open without heavy financial loss in spite of various schemes of retrenchment, and it was finally closed at the end of October Term 1917.

In September 1918 the officers of the O.U.T.C.[1]

[1] The Officers University Training Corps was started in 1917 and consisted of men from the ranks undergoing a course of six months' training at the University to prepare them for receiving commissions, and returning once more to the front as officers.

asked for the Club to be reopened for their use. The President and Treasurer therefore co-opted a Committee consisting of Mr Walter Durnford, Mr G. T. Lapsley and Mr Archibald Marshall to decide the matter. The Committee met early in October, and resolved to allow officers of the O.U.T.C. to become members of the Club, and, with the help of two representatives of the officers, they drew up a set of rules to regulate the membership. They also decided that "one or more billiard tables should be procured for the use of members, and that cards should be allowed at a low limit", and that "permission be asked of the Proctors to keep the Club open until 11 p.m." The Club actually opened on October 21st, a piano was placed in the dining room along with the two billiard tables and an inaugural concert was held on the 29th. A proposal was made that wives of members should be admitted to concerts either as performers or audience, but this was rejected by the Committee.

This period of the Club's activity was cut short by the signing of the Armistice, and at the beginning of the next term former members of the Club who had been serving in the army were beginning to come back into residence. Among these was Major Clarence Buxton, who had been elected Secretary in the May Term of 1914. He immediately and vigorously set to work to restore the Club to the life that it had known before the war.

On January 30th, 1919, Mr G. T. Lapsley entertained the Committee at their first meeting after the war to a dinner which, the Minutes say, "completely dispelled any anxieties as to the qualities of post bellum fare". The bitter-sweet to this dinner was the Treasurer's announcement that the attempts to keep the Club open during the war had left it £2600 in debt. Part of this debt was due to the O.U.T.C. having failed to provide the promised number of members: it was consequently decided to close the Club to members of this Corps at the end of the term. Sir Walter Durnford was then elected Deputy President as Mr Gaselee was not expected to return to Cambridge for some time, and a committee of undergraduates was also elected.

Later in this term there was a meeting of the Committee at which the Deputy President instructed the new members in their duties relating to the election of members of the Club, and the Treasurer and Secretary were requested to "restore the regimen of the Club to its pre-war standards of comfort and convenience especially in the matter of cuisine". The Treasurer said that they would have to proceed with caution while domestic difficulties were so great, but that he would see what Marshall, who was still steward, could do. It was, in fact, found impossible to open the dining room till the next term.

Under the able Secretaryship of G. K. Dunning (October 1919–March 1921) this restoration to pre-war standards of comfort and convenience proceeded rapidly, in spite of the resignation of Mr D. G. Marshall from the office of Steward owing to his decision to start a motor business. His loss might well have spelled disaster for the Club had not a worthy successor been found in Mr F. M. Hoppett, who had already been employed with occasional clerical work at the Club for fourteen years. Since his appointment the kitchen department has thrived, and he has been deservedly popular with each generation of post-war undergraduates that has known him.

The Committee meetings in 1920 were largely occupied with extensive elections, the number of members being increased to 200 owing to the enlarged state of the University. The Club had become nearly normal again, "the only real trouble", according to the Minutes, "being the horrible scarcity of whisky".

In June Marshall was given a silver rose bowl to mark the Club's appreciation of his services.

At the end of the October Term Mr Gaselee announced that he was shortly going to leave Cambridge to take up an appointment at the Foreign Office, and that he must consequently resign the Presidency. Mr E. M. Clark, Treasurer since 1905, was elected President and Mr R. H. Parker was elected Treasurer in his place.

From this time to the present the Club has continued to flourish. Its financial state improved so rapidly that in 1923 the Committee had already begun to discuss the possibility of alterations to the Club buildings. Mr C. W. Long, of Messrs Atkinson and Long, was asked to inspect the buildings and to draw up plans for improvements. His plans were soon completed and an estimate of £1400 to £1500 for their execution was presented to the Committee in May 1924. In discussing this estimate a division of opinion appeared. To carry out the work immediately would necessitate borrowing from the bank, which would add some £200 to the cost of the work itself, whereas in three years' time the Club would have the necessary cash. To postpone the work would thus save considerable extra expense but would prevent a whole generation of members from enjoying the improved rooms. Eventually by a majority of four to two it was decided to follow the proposal of the President and Treasurer and to have the work done immediately.

The alterations, delayed by a building strike, were eventually carried out in the Long Vacation of 1925. They consisted, as will be seen in Plan I*c*, chiefly in altering the position of the dining room and smoking room doors (the latter involving considerable alteration to the staircase), enlarging the Library, and moving the wash-basins to their present position.

A question of some historical interest was raised in June 1925, when a former secretary of the Club was entertained to dinner by the London Pitt Club, and a suggestion was made that the London secretary should be asked to dine at the University Pitt Club. The President was against this proposal and wrote to ask for the opinion of Sir Walter Fletcher, who replied: "...The London Pitt Club is a definitely political dining Club, belonging to the series of Pitt Clubs organised all over the country soon after Pitt's death. ...The Cambridge Club never had any relation to that series and has been purely social for at least sixty years. It would be a great mistake if it became in any way mixed up with the Political Pitt Clubs." The Committee followed this advice and the proposal was dropped.

At the beginning of 1927, plans for the redecoration of the dining room were discussed. There was great need for this improvement, for the room was draughty and uncomfortable. The floor was covered with the same linoleum that had served in Messrs Orme's billiard rooms, and was still pitted in the places in which the old tables had stood. In March 1927, following the sound principle "do it well or not at all", the Committee decided not to have the room merely replastered but to panel it in oak, and to have it done at once as the Club "could afford to carry out the scheme from every point of view". This did not mean that the Club had the necessary cash—indeed it was still in debt from the alterations of 1925—but that it was in such a prosperous condition that it would rapidly be able to pay off the overdraft which would be entailed.[1] Members have from time to time complained of the incurrence of so large an overdraft and of the rate of profit that its redemption necessarily involves: but there are few who are not grateful for their handsomely redecorated dining room and for their freedom from the inconveniences of the old room.

The work was carried out in the Long Vacation of

[1] The work in the dining room cost £1600. This raised the overdraft to £3700.

1927. A clock specially designed to stand over the sideboard was presented by the President. Later, a design for chairs for the room was approved by the Committee, and a scheme was started by which they could be presented by old and present members until the necessary number had been acquired.

In November 1929 the President expressed his wish to resign, and on December 1st the Rev. F. H. H. Clark, M.A., Fellow and Dean of Magdalene College, was elected to fill his place. The retiring President entertained Mr Clark and the rest of the Committee to dinner on December 4th and, in a farewell speech, declared his approval of the Committee's return to the old custom of having a don as president. He explained that he had been the only exception to this practice since it had started, and that he had only held the office as a result of the many disarrangements which the Great War had caused in university life.

On June 3rd, 1932, the Committee entertained to dinner the members of the delegation of Argentine Universities which was visiting Cambridge. They were also made honorary members of the Club during their visit.

In February 1933 General Sir Neill Malcolm, K.C.B., presented the Club with a large plaque of Pitt's head. It had formerly been on a wall at *The Bowling Green House*, Putney, Pitt's death-place, which was pulled down in 1932.[1] Later, the plaque was placed in the

[1] The plaque was advertised as "a bust of Chatham" and Sir Neill Malcolm bought it for Chatham House of which he was

The Club Rooms in Jesus Lane, 1935

centre of the pediment over the entrance to the Club.

In May 1933 Mr R. H. Parker, Treasurer since 1921, having announced his resignation, the Committee met and nominated as his successor Dr E. F. Collingwood, who was elected to the office at a general meeting of the Club on May 14th.

In the Long Vacation of 1933 the smoking room was furnished with new chairs and a reading desk, and an eighteenth-century round table was bought for the silence room.

On November 7th, 1933, a fire broke out in the neighbouring A.D.C. Theatre at 3 a.m. At 3.45 a.m. the Club was in danger, and some damage was done to the roof of the smoking room. It was found necessary to bring a hose through the hall of the Club and out by the manhole next to the washing room. Though effective in preventing any further spread of the fire, the hose was extremely leaky, and in spite of the efforts of the President, Treasurer, Secretary, the head-waiter and three policemen, who spent an hour sweeping water down to the drains in the basement, the floods did a certain amount of damage to the floors. The rooms could not be opened till luncheon time the next day, but there was no further interference with the normal life of the Club.

President. On delivery he immediately saw it represented the younger Pitt, not Chatham, and he therefore presented it to the U.P.C. It has not been found possible to discover any further details about its origin.

Of this normal life of the Club little has been said in the foregoing pages, although it is precisely this life that old members look back to with such affection. The Club rooms, whose remarkable development has been described, have themselves no importance except in that they have always been the ground for the making and meeting of friends. The rooms have changed, but the friendly spirit of the Club has remained unaltered for a hundred years, and it has therefore no history to be written. There is no reason for supposing that the next hundred years will see it change. There is certainly no reason for wishing it to do so.

VII

LIST OF OFFICERS AND COMMITTEES
1835—1935

THIS list has been compiled with the help of Mr H. Whitbread (U.P.C. 1931) from the Club's Minute Books. For the first three years of the Club's history there are no Minutes, but from an early receipt and from three summonses to Club meetings we have the names of the Treasurer of 1835, and of the Secretary of 1836. The Minutes for the years 1849–1868 are unfortunately lost. During these years, therefore, it is only possible to give the names of the Treasurers and Secretaries, derived from the "Treasurer's Book" of the period, and from the "List of Members", which was kept by the Secretary.

	Michaelmas 1835	
T. B. Charlton	Trinity	Treasurer

	Lent to Michaelmas 1836	
A. Watson	Corpus Christi	Secretary
C. Tower		Secretary

1837
(No records)

	Easter 1838	
F. R. Simpson	Queens'	President
H. Bullock	Christ's	Treasurer
Sir J. H. Lighton	St John's	Secretary
Lord John Manners	Trinity	
Hon. G. S. Smythe	St John's	
Hon. E. Herbert	St John's	

W. Stirling	Trinity	
F. G. Gregor	Trinity	
R. Bateson	Trinity	
F. Goulburn	Trinity	
B. W. Savile	Emmanuel	
J. P. Budworth	Jesus	
G. Jackson	Magdalene	

Michaelmas 1838

Hon. G. S. Smythe	St John's	President
C. S. Stokes	Trinity	Treasurer
Viscount Somerton	Trinity	Secretary
Lord John Manners	Trinity	
Hon. E. Herbert	St John's	
W. Stirling	Trinity	
F. Goulburn	Trinity	
J. P. Budworth	Jesus	
G. Jackson	Magdalene	
A. B. Hope	Trinity	
W. Massey	Trinity	
G. Goldney	King's	

Lent 1839

Hon. E. Herbert	St John's	President
C. S. Stokes	Trinity	Treasurer
Viscount Somerton	Trinity	Secretary
Hon. G. S. Smythe	St John's	
F. Goulburn	Trinity	
G. Jackson	Magdalene	
A. B. Hope	Trinity	
W. Massey	Trinity	
G. Goldney	King's	
Lord G. Manners	Trinity	
Sir S. H. Clarke	Trinity	
J. M. Balfour	Trinity	

Easter 1839

F. Goulburn	Trinity	President
C. S. Stokes	Trinity	Treasurer
Viscount Somerton	Trinity	Secretary
Hon. G. S. Smythe	St John's	
A. B. Hope	Trinity	
W. Massey	Trinity	
G. Goldney	King's	
Lord G. Manners	Trinity	

74

J. M. Balfour	Trinity	
Hon. E. Herbert	St John's	
F. Neville	Magdalene	
A. Cusack	Caius	

Michaelmas 1839

Viscount Somerton	Trinity	President
C. S. Stokes	Trinity	Treasurer
Hon. A. Savile	Trinity	Secretary
Hon. G. S. Smythe	St John's	
A. B. Hope	Trinity	
Lord Clive	St John's	
F. Neville	Magdalene	
Lord G. Manners	Trinity	
J. M. Balfour	Trinity	
T. I. Barstow	Trinity	
N. Fane	St John's	
J. P. Croft	Trinity	

Easter 1840

Viscount Somerton	Trinity	President
Hon. A. Savile	Trinity	Treasurer & Secretary
A. B. Hope	Trinity	
Lord G. Manners	Trinity	
J. M. Balfour	Trinity	
J. P. Croft	Trinity	
T. I. Barstow	Trinity	
G. F. Bentinck	Trinity	
Hon. C. Vereker	Trinity	
N. Fane	St John's	

Michaelmas 1840

Hon. A. Savile	Trinity	President
G. F. Bentinck	Trinity	Treasurer
R. Winn	Trinity	Secretary
T. I. Barstow	Trinity	
J. Gillbanks	St John's	
A. Lowther	Trinity	
W. T. Bullock	Caius	
F. A. Goulburn	Trinity	
H. Pix	Emmanuel	
J. Lonsdale	Trinity	
J. Banks	Christ's	
R. Hamilton	Trinity	

	Lent 1841	
A. Lowther	Trinity	President
G. F. Bentinck	Trinity	Treasurer
J. M. Ridley	Jesus	Secretary
J. Gillbanks	St John's	
W. T. Bullock	Caius	
H. Pix	Emmanuel	
J. Banks	Christ's	
R. Hamilton	Trinity	
G. H. Hodson	Trinity	
A. H. Hope	Trinity	
C. R. Lighton	St John's	
B. Smith	Peterhouse	

	Easter 1841	
A. Lowther	Trinity	President
G. F. Bentinck	Trinity	Treasurer
R. Winn	Trinity	Secretary
J. M. Ridley	Jesus	
J. Gillbanks	St John's	
W. T. Bullock	Caius	
R. Hamilton	Trinity	
G. H. Hodson	Trinity	
C. R. Lighton	St John's	
B. Smith	Peterhouse	
J. G. Lonsdale	Trinity	
T. L. French	Emmanuel	

	Michaelmas 1841 *to Easter* 1842	
G. F. Bentinck	Trinity	President
G. H. Hodson	Trinity	Treasurer
J. Gillbanks	St John's	Secretary
B. Smith	Peterhouse	M.
R. Hamilton	Trinity	M.
W. T. Bullock	Caius	M. & L.
C. R. Lighton	St John's	M. & L.
J. M. Ridley	Jesus	M. & L.
T. L. French	Emmanuel	
A. Lowther	Trinity	
J. M. Campbell	Trinity	
B. Burton	Magdalene	
T. I. Barstow	Trinity	
T. Robinson	Trinity	L. & E.
R. B. Blackburn	Trinity	L. & E.
Earl Nelson	Trinity	E.
F. Peel	Trinity	E.
J. G. Beresford	Peterhouse	E.

76

Michaelmas 1842 to Easter 1843

Earl Nelson	Trinity	President
T. Robinson	Trinity	Treasurer
T. L. French	Emmanuel	Secretary
G. F. Bentinck	Trinity	M.
A. Lowther	Trinity	M.
R. B. Blackburn	Trinity	M.
J. Gillbanks	St John's	M. & E.
F. Peel	Trinity	
J. G. Beresford	Peterhouse	
W. S. Hodson	Trinity	
F. Boscawen	Magdalene	
C. Morse	Trinity	
Viscount Fielding	Trinity	L. & E.
R. Clive	St John's	L. & E.
E. T. Henry	Caius	L. & E.
Hon. G. T. O. Bridgeman	Trinity	E.

Michaelmas 1843 to Easter 1844

Viscount Fielding	Trinity	President M. & E.
T. Robinson	Trinity	Treasurer
R. Clive	St John's	Secretary
Earl of Gifford	Trinity	President E.
Earl Nelson	Trinity	M.
J. G. Beresford	Peterhouse	M.
W. S. Hodson	Trinity	M.
T. L. French	Emmanuel	M. & L.
T. T. Boscawen	Magdalene	
F. Peel	Trinity	
Hon. G. T. O. Bridgeman	Trinity	
Hon. F. Grimston	Magdalene	
Hon. D. Gordon	Trinity	L. & E.
T. Sapte	Emmanuel	L. & E.
G. Hazelrigg	St John's	L. & E.
T. W. Brooks	Trinity	E.
E. H. Loring	Trinity	E.

Michaelmas 1844

Earl of Gifford	Trinity	President
C. J. Ellicott	St John's	Treasurer
Hon. D. Gordon	Trinity	Secretary
Hon. F. Grimston	Magdalene	
T. Sapte	Emmanuel	
G. Hazlerigg	St John's	
T. W. Brooks	Trinity	
E. H. Loring	St John's	

T. T. Boscawen	Magdalene	
C. Gordon	Peterhouse	
J. G. C. Russell	Trinity	

Lent and Easter 1845

T. T. Boscawen	Magdalene	President
J. G. C. Russell	Trinity	Treasurer
Hon. D. Gordon	Trinity	Secretary
Hon. F. Grimston	Magdalene	L.
G. Hazelrigg	St John's	L.
G. F. Egerton	Trinity	L.
Lord Burghley	St John's	
W. Harkness	St John's	
C. G. Hill	Trinity	
T. H. Standen	Trinity	
H. T. Holland	Trinity	
G. F. Murdoch	St John's	
C. Gordon	Peterhouse	
R. E. Hughes	Magdalene	E.
R. A. Cross	Trinity	E.

Michaelmas 1845

Lord Burghley	St John's	President
R. A. Cross	Trinity	Treasurer
H. T. Holland	Trinity	Secretary
T. T. Boscawen	Magdalene	
C. G. Hill	Trinity	
G. F. Murdoch	St John's	
Hon. D. Gordon	Trinity	
C. Gordon	Peterhouse	
F. French	Peterhouse	
W. Harkness	St John's	
T. H. Standen	Trinity	
R. E. Hughes	Magdalene	

Lent and Easter 1846

G. F. Murdoch	St John's	Secretary

Michaelmas 1846

F. French	Peterhouse	Treasurer
G. F. Murdoch	St John's	Secretary

The names of the full Committees for the year 1846 cannot be given, for the Secretary for that year "neglected to insert minutes of the proceedings during that time". But there is a note saying that "Mr Coles (G.R.), Magdalene, and Mr Cotton (A.O.), Jesus, were elected members of the committee".

	Lent 1847	
Hon. G. Herbert	St John's	President
R. E. Hughes	Magdalene	Treasurer
G. F. Murdoch	St John's	Secretary
G. W. Horton	Trinity	
A. D. Veasey	Trinity	
T. W. Wiglesworth	Caius	
Hon. L. Neville	Magdalene	
T. Cook	Magdalene	
S. Lloyd	St John's	
—. Watson	Trinity Hall	

	Easter 1847	
R. E. Hughes	Magdalene	President
G. W. Horton	Trinity	Treasurer
Hon. L. Neville	Magdalene	Secretary
T. Cook	Magdalene	
A. D. Veasey	Trinity	
T. W. Wiglesworth	Caius	
S. W. Lloyd	St John's	
R. Harkness	St John's	
E. N. Crake	Trinity	
C. Soames	Caius	
—. Watson	Trinity Hall	

	Michaelmas 1847 *to Easter* 1848	
R. E. Hughes	Magdalene	President
Hon. L. Neville	Magdalene	Treasurer
T. W. Wiglesworth	Caius	Secretary
A. D. Veasey	Trinity	M.
R. Harkness	St John's	M.
S. W. Lloyd	St John's	
E. N. Crake	Trinity	
C. Soames	Caius	
C. O. Eaton	Trinity	
R. W. Tollemache	Peterhouse	
—. Grimston	Trinity Hall	
G. F. Holroyd	Trinity	L. & E.
E. Barchard	Trinity	L. & E.
Hon. G. Gifford	Caius	L. & E.
H. W. Jones	Trinity	E.

	Michaelmas 1848	
R. E. Hughes	Magdalene	President
G. F. Holroyd	Trinity	Treasurer
A. D. Veasey	Trinity	Secretary

H. W. Jones	Trinity
W. H. Hand	Jesus
C. B. Marlay	Trinity
C. Jenkins	Magdalene
Jervoise Smith	Trinity
R. V. Blathwayt	Trinity
Hon. L. Neville	Magdalene

Samuel Jackson of Magdalene succeeded R. E. Hughes and was President till the move in 1866, when R. C. Jebb of Trinity succeeded him. From 1849–68, the offices of Treasurer and Secretary were held by the following members:

		TREASURER	SECRETARY
1848	M. }	G. F. Holroyd	A. D. Veasey
1849	L.E. }	Trinity	Trinity
	M. }	,,	Gervoise Smith
1850	L.E. }		Trinity
	M. }	G. F. Holroyd	A. de Rutzen
1851	L.E. }	Trinity	Trinity
	M. }	C. B. Marlay	Alfred Newton
1852	L.E. }	Trinity	Magdalene
	M. }	,,	E. Macnaghten
1853	L.E. }		Trinity
	M.	A. Bramwell	G. P. M. Campbell
		Trinity	Magdalene
1854	L.E.	A. C. Walford	
		Trinity	,,
	M.	,,	W. Wyndham Neville
			Magdalene
1855	L.E.M.	H. Schreiber	,,
		Trinity Hall	
1856	L.	,,	
	E.	,,	C. W. Markham
			Magdalene
	M.	W. Hawthorn	H. Schreiber
		Trinity	Trinity Hall
1857	L.E.M.	,,	
1858	L.E.	R. L. Lloyd	J. L. Wharton
		Trinity	Trinity
	M. }	,,	,,
1859	L.E. }		
	M. }	John Hall	J. T. Morland
1860	L.E.M. }	Magdalene	Trinity
1861	L.	,,	John Hall
			Magdalene
	E.	Leslie Stephen	W. Henty
		Trinity Hall	Trinity

Year		TREASURER	SECRETARY
1861	M.	Leslie Stephen Trinity Hall	T. F. Kirby Trinity
1862	L.E.M.	,,	,,
1863	L.E.M.	,,	,,
1864	L.E.	,,	,,
	M.	H. J. Fortescue Magdalene	,,
1865	L.E.	,,	,,
	M.	,,	G. H. Tuck Trinity
1866	L.	,,	A. Pope Trinity
	E.	J. Reid Trinity	
1867	M. L.E. }	,,	M. Sim Trinity
1868	M. L.E. }	W. Durnford King's	C. Pitt-Taylor[1] Trinity

Lent and Easter 1869

R. C. Jebb, M.A.	Trinity	President
W. Durnford	King's	Treasurer
C. E. Oldman	Trinity	Secretary
C. E. Knight	Trinity Hall	Librarian
S. F. Akroyd	Trinity	L.
F. H. Hunt	Trinity	
E. Royds	Trinity Hall	
A. C. Ryder	St John's	
J. B. Humfrey	Trinity	
H. H. Stewart	Trinity	E.

Michaelmas 1869 *to Michaelmas* 1870

R. C. Jebb, M.A.	Trinity	President
W. Durnford	King's	Treasurer
H. H. Stewart	Trinity	Secretary
C. B. Bruce	Trinity	Librarian
E. Royds	Trinity Hall	
H. R. Hunt	Trinity Hall	
R. I. Blackburne	Trinity	
E. S. L. Randolph	Trinity	
C. G. Walpole	Trinity	
A. P. Maudesley	Trinity Hall	
J. H. D. Goldie	St John's	

[1] The names of three other members of the Committee of this year are given with the photograph facing p. 38.

Lent and Easter 1871

R. C. Jebb, M.A.	Trinity	President
W. Durnford	King's	Treasurer
E. S. L. Randolph	Trinity	Secretary
A. P. Maudesley	Trinity Hall	Librarian
C. B. Bruce	Trinity	
C. G. Walpole	Trinity	L.
E. Royds	Trinity Hall	
J. H. D. Goldie	St John's	
H. P. Laing	St John's	
A. H. Delme-Radcliffe	Trinity	
H. E. Jones	Trinity Hall	
G. E. Welby	Trinity	E.

Michaelmas 1871 to Easter 1872

R. C. Jebb, M.A.	Trinity	President
J. H. D. Goldie	St John's	Treasurer
G. E. Welby	Trinity	Secretary
A. P. Maudesley	Trinity Hall	Librarian
C. B. Bruce	Trinity	
H. P. Laing	St John's	M.
A. H. Delme-Radcliffe	Trinity	
H. A. Macnaughten	King's	
C. S. Maine	Trinity	
J. J. Reubell	Trinity Hall	
H. Neville	Magdalene	L. & E.
Hon. A. T. Lyttleton	Trinity	E.

Michaelmas 1872 to Easter 1873

R. C. Jebb, M.A.	Trinity	President
Hon. A. T. Lyttelton	Trinity	Treasurer
H. Neville	Magdalene	Secretary
J. J. Reubell	Trinity Hall	Librarian
A. H. Delme-Radcliffe	Trinity	
C. W. Benson	Trinity	
Viscount Stopford	Trinity	
G. Macan	Trinity Hall	
N. E. Muggeridge	King's	
W. H. Fawkes	St John's	
J. F. Brocklehurst	Trinity	L. & E.
A. Crossley	Trinity	E.

Michaelmas 1873

R. C. Jebb, M.A.	Trinity	President
Hon. A. T. Lyttelton	Trinity	Treasurer
G. Macan	Trinity Hall	Secretary

A. Crossley	Trinity	
R. B. Brett	Trinity	
Viscount Ebrington	Trinity	
C. Tillard	Clare	
A. A. Tilley	King's	
W. H. Fawkes	St John's	
J. F. Brocklehurst	Trinity	

Lent and Easter 1874

R. C. Jebb, M.A.	Trinity	President
G. Macan	Trinity Hall	Treasurer
A. A. Tilley	King's	Secretary
R. B. Brett	Trinity	Librarian L.
A. S. Tabor	Trinity	Librarian E.
Viscount Ebrington	Trinity	L.
C. Tillard	Clare	L.
A. Crossley	Trinity	
B. H. Buxton	Trinity	
J. A. Campbell	Trinity Hall	
W. Blacker	Downing	E.
J. E. Peabody	Trinity	E.
Hon. A. H. Henniker-Major	Magdalene	E.

Michaelmas 1874

R. C. Jebb, M.A.	Trinity	President
G. Macan	Trinity Hall	Treasurer
A. A. Tilley	King's	Secretary
A. S. Tabor	Trinity	Librarian
A. Crossley	Trinity	
Viscount Ebrington	Trinity	
J. E. Peabody	Trinity	
W. Blacker	Downing	
Hon. A. H. Henniker-Major	Magdalene	
G. H. Longman	Trinity	

Lent and Easter 1875

R. C. Jebb, M.A.	Trinity	President
Viscount Ebrington	Trinity	Treasurer
A. A. Tilley	King's	Secretary L.
J. E. Peabody	Trinity	Librarian L.
J. T. Penrose	Trinity	Secretary E.
Hon. A. H. Bourke	Trinity	Librarian E.

Lent and Easter 1875 (cont.)

R. Woodhouse	Trinity	
A. T. Olive	Trinity Hall	
C. R. Carew	St John's	
G. R. Murray	Trinity	E.
S. G. Holland	Trinity Hall	E.

Michaelmas 1875

R. C. Jebb, M.A.	Trinity	President
A. T. Olive	Trinity Hall	Treasurer
J. T. Penrose	Trinity	Secretary
Hon. A. H. Bourke	Trinity	Librarian
C. R. Carew	St John's	
S. G. Holland	Trinity Hall	
C. D. Shafto	Jesus	
F. H. Mellor	Trinity	
M. Frewen	Trinity	
P. E. Crutchley	Trinity	

Lent and Easter 1876

J. Prior, M.A.	Trinity	President
J. T. Penrose	Trinity	Treasurer
S. G. Holland	Trinity Hall	Secretary
Hon. A. H. Bourke	Trinity	Librarian L.
F. H. Mellor	Trinity	Librarian E.
C. D. Shafto	Jesus	
M. Frewen	Trinity	
P. E. Crutchley	Trinity	
E. W. Collin	King's	
C. Thornhill	Magdalene	

Michaelmas 1876 to Lent 1877

J. Prior, M.A.	Trinity	President
F. H. Mellor	Trinity	Treasurer
S. G. Holland	Trinity Hall	Secretary M.
P. E. Crutchley	Trinity	Secretary L.
Hon. E. Lyttelton	Trinity	Librarian
C. Thornhill	Magdalene	
E. W. Collin	King's	
R. C. Lehmann	Trinity	
A. W. Pulteney	Trinity	
A. E. Fellowes	Trinity Hall	
A. Holland Hibbert	Trinity Hall	L.

Easter and Michaelmas 1877

J. Prior, M.A.	Trinity	President
P. E. Crutchley	Trinity	Treasurer
E. W. Collin	King's	Secretary
Hon. E. Lyttelton	Trinity	Librarian
C. Thornhill	Magdalene	
R. C. Lehmann	Trinity	
A. W. Pulteney	Trinity	
A. E. Fellowes	Trinity Hall	
A. Holland Hibbert	Trinity Hall	E.
C. E. Gurdon	Jesus	
Hon. A. G. Lawley	Trinity	M.

Lent 1878

J. Prior, M.A.	Trinity	President
A. W. Pulteney	Trinity	Treasurer
E. W. Collin	King's	Secretary
Hon. E. Lyttelton	Trinity	Librarian
R. C. Lehmann	Trinity	
C. E. Gurdon	Jesus	
Hon. A. G. Lawley	Trinity	
G. O. P. Bouverie	Trinity	
H. T. Coles	Trinity Hall	
H. R. Magniac	Magdalene	

Easter and Michaelmas 1878

J. Prior, M.A.	Trinity	President
A. W. Pulteney	Trinity	Treasurer E.
E. Peabody	Trinity	Treasurer M.
Hon. A. G. Lawley	Trinity	Secretary
E. O. P. Bouverie	Trinity	Librarian
H. T. Coles	Trinity Hall	Auditor
H. R. Magniac	Magdalene	
C. M. Newton	King's	
Hon. A. Lyttelton	Trinity	
W. H. Churchill	Jesus	
L. K. Jervis	Trinity	

Lent and Easter 1879

J. Prior, M.A.	Trinity	President
E. Peabody	Trinity	Treasurer
L. K. Jervis	Trinity	Secretary
C. M. Newton	King's	Librarian
H. T. Coles	Trinity Hall	Auditor

H. R. Magniac	Magdalene
Hon. R. O. A. Milnes	Trinity
F. Gelderd	Jesus
Hon. I. F. Bligh	Trinity
S. H. Whitbread	Trinity

Michaelmas 1879

J. Prior, M.A.	Trinity	President
E. Peabody	Trinity	Treasurer
H. R. Magniac	Magdalene	Secretary
Hon. R. O. A. Milnes	Trinity	Librarian
F. Gelderd	Jesus	Auditor
Hon. I. F. Bligh	Trinity	
S. H. Whitbread	Trinity	
A. G. Steel	Trinity Hall	
C. W. Foley	King's	
T. K. Tapling	Trinity	

Lent 1880

J. Prior, M.A.	Trinity	President
Hon. I. F. Bligh	Trinity	Treasurer
H. R. Magniac	Magdalene	Secretary
T. K. Tapling	Trinity	Librarian
F. Gelderd	Jesus	Auditor
A. G. Steel	Trinity Hall	
C. W. Foley	King's	
A. Nimmo	Trinity	
E. D. L. Harvey	Trinity	
H. Whitfield	Trinity	

Easter 1880

J. Prior, M.A.	Trinity	President
F. Gelderd	Jesus	Treasurer
Hon. I. F. Bligh	Trinity	Secretary
T. K. Tapling	Trinity	Librarian
A. G. Steel	Trinity Hall	Auditor
C. W. Foley	King's	
A. Nimmo	Trinity	
E. D. L. Harvey	Trinity	
H. Whitfield	Trinity	

N.B. After Easter 1880 the membership of the Committee throughout each academic year varies considerably less than in earlier years. From this date, therefore, all members who served for any period in the academic year are here put in one list; and only the variations from term to term of officers are noted in the margin.

From 1880 onwards the Secretary ranks above the Treasurer, reversing the order of the preceding years.

Michaelmas 1880 *to Easter* 1881

J. Prior, M.A.	Trinity	President
Hon. I. F. Bligh	Trinity	Secretary M.
F. Geldard	Jesus	Treasurer M.
A. Nimmo	Trinity	Librarian M. & L.
Hon. J. ff. Wallop	Trinity	Auditor M., Secretary L. & E.
J. A. Watson Taylor	Magdalene	Treasurer L. & E.
H. F. B. Thynne	King's	Auditor L. & E.
W. G. Elliot	Trinity	Librarian E.
E. D. L. Harvey	Trinity	
E. M. Lawson-Smith	Trinity	
E. C. Brooksbank	Trinity Hall	
G. M. Smith	Jesus	
F. W. Leaf	Trinity	

Michaelmas 1881 *to Easter* 1882

J. Prior, M.A.	Trinity	President
W. G. Elliot	Trinity	Secretary M.
F. W. Leaf	Trinity	Treasurer M.
E. M. Lawson-Smith	Trinity	Librarian M., Secretary L. & E.
H. F. B. Thynne	King's	Auditor M.
H. H. Birley	Jesus	Treasurer L. & E.
J. Drinkwater-Lawe	Trinity Hall	Auditor L. & E.
A. E. Green-Price	Trinity	Librarian L. & E.
G. Streatfield	Trinity	
R. Hunt	Magdalene	
C. T. Studd	Trinity	
A. Macnamara	Trinity	
F. B. Mildmay	Trinity	
R. H. Macaulay	King's	
E. Impey	King's	

Michaelmas 1882 *to Easter* 1883

J. Prior, M.A.	Trinity	President
A. Macnamara	Trinity	Secretary
F. B. Mildmay	Trinity	Treasurer
E. Impey	King's	Librarian
F. G. L. Lucas	Trinity	Auditor

87

Michaelmas 1882 *to Easter* 1883 (*cont.*)

F. Straker	Jesus
F. C. Meyrick	Trinity Hall
G. A. St J. Mildmay	Magdalene
E. H. Hardcastle	Trinity
J. E. K. Studd	Trinity

Michaelmas 1883 *to Easter* 1884

Rev. F. Gunton, M.A.	Magdalene	President
J. E. K. Studd	Trinity	Secretary M.
F. Straker	Jesus	Treasurer M., Secretary L. & E.
G. Buxton	Trinity	Librarian M., Treasurer L. & E.
Hon. J. Mansfield	Trinity	Auditor M., Librarian L. & E.
G. W. E. Loder	Trinity	Auditor L. & E.
F. M. Ogilvie	King's	
W. G. Nicholson	Trinity	
W. Hollins	Trinity Hall	
Hon. A. W. Willoughby	Magdalene	
St C. G. A. Donaldson	Trinity	
Hon. L. F. Tyrwhitt	Magdalene	

Michaelmas 1884 *to Easter* 1885

Rev. F. Gunton, M.A.	Magdalene	President
F. Straker	Jesus	Secretary M.
G. W. E. Loder	Trinity	Treasurer M.
St C. G. A. Donaldson	Trinity	Librarian M., Secretary L. & E.
Hon. L. F. Tyrwhitt	Magdalene	Auditor M., Treasurer L.
J. A. Turner	Trinity	Librarian L., Treasurer E.
P. T. Davies Cooke	Trinity Hall	Auditor L., Librarian E.
L. Sanderson	Trinity	Auditor E.
W. Moncreiffe	Trinity	
C. A. C. Birch	King's	
C. D. Seymour	Jesus	
H. W. Bainbridge	Trinity	
M. R. James	King's	
Hon. M. B. Hawke	Magdalene	

Michaelmas 1885 *to Easter* 1886

Rev. F. Gunton, M.A.	Magdalene	President
H. W. Bainbridge	Trinity	Secretary
M. R. James	King's	Treasurer
C. D. Seymour	Jesus	Librarian M. & L.
F. J. Pitman	Trinity	Auditor
C. D. Buxton	Trinity	Librarian E.
Hon. L. F. Tyrwhitt	Magdalene	
C. H. Leaf	Trinity	
D. Cunliffe-Smith	Trinity Hall	
T. Greatorex	Trinity	

Michaelmas 1886 *to Easter* 1887

Rev. F. Gunton, M.A.	Magdalene	President M. & L.
C. H. Leaf	Trinity	Secretary M.
C. D. Buxton	Trinity	Treasurer M., Secretary L. & E.
W. C. Bridgeman	Trinity	Librarian
Hon. C. M. Knachbull-Hugessen	King's	Auditor M.
H. E. Crawley	Trinity	Treasurer L. & E.
L. G. B. J. Ford	King's	Auditor L. & E.
M. R. James, B.A.	King's	President E.
R. O. Ridley	Trinity Hall	
S. D. Muttlebury	Trinity	
Hon. L. E. Lowther	Magdalene	
H. S. A. Sanford	Jesus	
G. Kemp	Trinity	
G. M. Rutherford	Magdalene	

Michaelmas 1887 *to Easter* 1888

M. R. James, B.A.	King's	President
W. C. Bridgeman	Trinity	Secretary M.
R. O. Ridley	Trinity Hall	Treasurer
L. G. B. J. Ford	King's	Librarian
S. D. Muttlebury	Trinity	Auditor M., Secretary L. & E.
E. Crawley	Trinity	
M. P. Parker	Trinity	
H. F. Hayhurst	Trinity	
H. S. A. Sanford	Jesus	
G. M. Rutherford	Magdalene	
B. R. Warren	Trinity	
Hon. H. A. Milles	Trinity Hall	
C. C. Williams	Magdalene	
F. G. J. Ford	King's	

Michaelmas 1888 *to Easter* 1889

M. R. James, B.A.	King's	President
S. D. Muttlebury	Trinity	Secretary
E. M. Butler	Trinity	Treasurer
F. G. J. Ford	King's	Librarian
Hon. H. A. Milles	Trinity Hall	Auditor
B. R. Warren	Trinity	
C. C. Williams	Magdalene	
W. I. Rowell	Jesus	
Hon. G. H. D. Willoughby	Trinity	
G. H. Cotterill	Trinity	

Michaelmas 1889 *to Easter* 1890

M. R. James, M.A.	King's	President
S. D. Muttlebury	Trinity	Secretary
G. H. Cotterill	Trinity	Treasurer
W. I. Rowell	Jesus	Librarian
W. H. Leese	Trinity	Auditor
L. MacCreery	Magdalene	
V. C. W. Cavendish	Trinity	
H.H. Prince F. Duleep Singh	Magdalene	
W. Whitelaw	Trinity	
A. Bailey	Trinity Hall	
A. F. Smith	Trinity Hall	

Michaelmas 1890 *to Easter* 1891

M. R. James, M.A.	King's	President
V. C. W. Cavendish	Trinity	Secretary M.
L. MacCreery	Magdalene	Treasurer
G. T. Foljambe	Trinity	Librarian M., Secretary L. & E.
G. E. R. Elin	Trinity	Auditor
C. H. O. Dennistoun	Trinity Hall	Librarian L. & E.
E. C. Grenfell	Trinity	
F. S. Jackson	Trinity	
A. J. L. Hill	Jesus	
S. F. Wombwell	Trinity Hall	
O. Hugh Smith	Trinity	

Michaelmas 1891 *to Easter* 1892

M. R. James, M.A.	King's	President
G. E. R. Elin	Trinity	Secretary
E. C. Grenfell	Trinity	Treasurer

Michaelmas 1891 *to Easter* 1892 *(cont.)*

F. S. Jackson	Trinity	Librarian
A. J. L. Hill	Jesus	Auditor
A. B. Marten	Trinity	
R. F. Cavendish	Trinity	
G. Heseltine	Trinity Hall	
S. F. Wombwell	Trinity Hall	
E. L. Churchill	King's	

Michaelmas 1892 *to Easter* 1893

M. R. James, M.A.	King's	President
A. B. Marten	Trinity	Secretary
C. G. Pope	Trinity	Treasurer
T. G. E. Lewis	Trinity	Librarian
R. E. Holland	Trinity	Auditor
G. Heseltine	Trinity Hall	
Hon. I. C. Guest	Trinity	
M. J. L. Beebee	King's	
Hon. M. G. Tollemache	Trinity	
H. R. Bromley Davenport	Trinity Hall	

Michaelmas 1893 *to Easter* 1894

M. R. James, M.A.	King's	President
C. G. Pope	Trinity	Secretary
T. G. E. Lewis	Trinity	Treasurer
R. C. Norman	Trinity	Librarian
C. J. L. Rudd	Trinity	Auditor
T. B. Hope	Trinity Hall	
J. B. Pelham	Trinity	
R. A. Austen Leigh	King's	
R. O. Kerrison	Trinity	
J. M. Dawson	Trinity Hall	

Michaelmas 1894 *to Easter* 1895

M. R. James, Litt.D.	King's	President
C. G. Pope	Trinity	Secretary
C. J. L. Rudd	Trinity	Treasurer
T. B. Hope	Trinity Hall	Librarian
R. A. Austen Leigh	King's	Auditor
E. H. Bonham	Trinity	
R. A. Studd	Trinity	
E. Talbot	Trinity	
J. S. Cavendish	Trinity	
F. Hargreaves	Trinity Hall	
W. G. Druce	Trinity	

91

Michaelmas 1895 *to Easter* 1896

M. R. James, Litt.D.	King's	President
C. J. L. Rudd	Trinity	Secretary M. & E.
T. B. Hope	Trinity Hall	Treasurer M. & L.
E. Talbot	Trinity	Librarian
Hon. O. Bridgeman	Trinity	Auditor M. & L., Treasurer E.
C. W. H. Rodwell	King's	Secretary L.
P. W. Cobbold	Trinity	Auditor E.
W. H. Allen	Trinity	
H. M. Bland	Trinity	
F. M. Freake	Magdalene	
A. S. Bell	Trinity Hall	

Michaelmas 1896 *to Easter* 1897

M. R. James, Litt.D.	King's	President
Hon. O. Bridgeman	Trinity	Secretary M.
W. H. Allen	Trinity	Treasurer M.
C. W. H. Rodwell	King's	Librarian M.
H. M. Bland	Trinity	Auditor M., Secretary L.
A. S. Bell	Trinity Hall	Treasurer L. & E.
A. R. Jelf	King's	Librarian L. & E.
C. V. Brooke	Magdalene	Auditor L., Secretary E.
J. H. Bullock	Trinity	Auditor E.
A. L. Harrison	Trinity	
Earl of Ronaldshay	Trinity	
J. A. Crocker	Trinity	
Earl of Lytton	Trinity	
A. H. Gibbs	Trinity Hall	
J. P. Barber	Trinity	

Michaelmas 1897 *to Easter* 1898

M. R. James, Litt.D.	King's	President
Earl of Lytton	Trinity	Secretary
A. S. Bell	Trinity Hall	Treasurer
H. W. de Zoete	Trinity	Librarian
J. A. Crocker	Trinity	Auditor
J. H. Stogden	Trinity	
L. W. Ogilvy	King's	
W. Dudley Ward	Trinity	
Lord Hindlip	Trinity	
D. E. Campbell Muir	Trinity Hall	
C. E. M. Wilson	Trinity	

Michaelmas 1898 to Easter 1899

M. R. James, Litt.D.	King's	President
L. W. Ogilvy	King's	Secretary
H. A. Arkwright	Trinity	Treasurer M. & L.
W. Dudley Ward	Trinity	Librarian
R. B. Etherington-Smith	Trinity	Auditor
E. H. Parker, M.A.	King's	Treasurer E.
W. N. Pilkington	Trinity	
C. J. D. Goldie	Trinity	
L. O. T. Baines	Trinity Hall	
J. C. Tabor	Trinity	
T. G. C. Cole	Trinity Hall	

Michaelmas 1899 to Easter 1900

W. M. Fletcher, M.A.	Trinity	President
W. Dudley Ward	Trinity	Secretary
E. H. Parker, M.A.	King's	Treasurer
T. G. C. Cole	Trinity Hall	Librarian
C. J. D. Goldie	Trinity	Auditor
A. Hunter	Trinity	
E. O. Lewin	King's	
G. L. Lyon	Trinity	
H. M. Burroughes	Trinity	
W. G. Paget-Tomlinson	Trinity Hall	
W. P. Robertson	Trinity Hall	
H. G. Leith	Trinity	

Michaelmas 1900 to Easter 1901

W. M. Fletcher, M.A.	Trinity	President
W. Dudley Ward	Trinity	Secretary M.
E. H. Parker, M.A.	King's	Treasurer
Viscount Howick	Trinity	Librarian M., Secretary L. & E.
B. W. D. Brooke	Trinity	Auditor M.
W. Hedley	King's	Librarian L. & E.
E. M. Dowson	Trinity	Auditor L. & E.
W. P. Robertson	Trinity Hall	
G. McD. Maitland	Trinity	
O. B. Pease	Trinity Hall	
C. W. H. Taylor	Trinity	
C. H. Ebden	Trinity	
H. B. Grylls	Trinity	

W. M. Fletcher, M.A.	Trinity	President
W. Hedley	King's	Secretary
E. H. Parker, M.A.	King's	Treasurer
C. W. H. Taylor	Trinity	Librarian
W. H. Chapman	Trinity	Auditor
E. M. Dowson	Trinity	
C. H. Ebden	Trinity	
H. B. Grylls	Trinity	
N. O. Tagart	Jesus	
P. L. Hollins	Trinity Hall	
C. B. L. Tennyson	King's	

Michaelmas 1902 *to Easter* 1903

W. M. Fletcher, M.A.	Trinity	President
W. H. Chapman	Trinity	Secretary
E. H. Parker, M.A.	King's	Treasurer
C. B. L. Tennyson	King's	Librarian
R. H. Nelson	Trinity	Auditor
A. Buxton	Trinity	
J. S. Carter	King's	
J. Churchill	Trinity	
H. P. Croft	Trinity Hall	
E. J. McCorquodale	Trinity	

Michaelmas 1903 *to Easter* 1904

W. M. Fletcher, M.A.	Trinity	President
R. H. Nelson	Trinity	Secretary M.
E. H. Parker, M.A.	King's	Treasurer
A. Buxton	Trinity	Librarian M., Secretary L. & E.
J. Edwards-Moss	Trinity	Auditor
Hon. G. W. Lyttelton	Trinity	Librarian L. & E.
C. G. Hoare	King's	
E. W. Mann	Trinity	
G. C. Agnew	King's	
Lord Wodehouse	Trinity Hall	
S. Gaselee	King's	
H. L. Sheppard	Trinity Hall	

Michaelmas 1904 *to Easter* 1905

W. M. Fletcher, M.A.	Trinity	President
C. G. Hoare	King's	Secretary M. & L.
E. H. Parker, M.A.	King's	Treasurer M.

Michaelmas 1904 to Easter 1905 (cont.)

Hon. G. W. Lyttelton	Trinity	Librarian M. & L., Secretary E.
Lord Wodehouse	Trinity Hall	Auditor
E. M. Clark, M.A.	Trinity	Treasurer L. & E.
S. Gaselee	King's	Librarian E.
B. C. Johnstone	Trinity	
Hon. I. M. Campbell	Trinity	
N. A. C. Flower	Trinity	
C. H. Deane	Trinity	
H. C. McDonell	Corpus Christi	

Michaelmas 1905 to Easter 1906

W. M. Fletcher, M.A.	Trinity	President
Hon. G. W. Lyttelton	Trinity	Secretary
E. M. Clark, M.A.	Trinity	Treasurer
C. H. Deane	Trinity	Librarian
Hon. I. M. Campbell	Trinity	Auditor M.
N. A. C. Flower	Trinity	
H. F. P. Hearson	King's	
S. M. Bruce	Trinity Hall	
F. J. V. Hopley	Pembroke	
Hon. R. A. Fellowes	Trinity	
R. P. Birchenough	Trinity Hall	
H. B. Gething	Trinity	
E. H. Ryle	Trinity	
R. V. Powell	Trinity	

Michaelmas 1906 to Easter 1907

W. M. Fletcher, M.A.	Trinity	President
H. F. P. Hearson	King's	Secretary
E. M. Clark, M.A.	Trinity	Treasurer
E. H. Ryle	Trinity	Librarian
R. P. Birchenough	Trinity Hall	Auditor
Hon. R. A. Fellowes	Trinity	
Hon. B. B. Ponsonby	Trinity	
E. W. Powell	Trinity	
J. N. Buchanan	Trinity	
R. C. Simpson	Trinity	
Hon. C. F. Lyttelton	Trinity	
R. S. Durnford	King's	
E. A. de Rothschild	Trinity	

Michaelmas 1907 *to Easter* 1908

W. M. Fletcher, M.A.	Trinity	President
E. H. Ryle	Trinity	Secretary
E. M. Clark, M.A.	Trinity	Treasurer
R. S. Durnford	King's	Librarian
J. N. Buchanan	Trinity	Auditor
E. W. Powell	Trinity	
Hon. C. F. Lyttelton	Trinity	
M. C. Albright	Trinity	
V. G. Thew	Trinity Hall	
A. W. M. S. Griffin	Trinity	

Michaelmas 1908 *to Easter* 1909

W. M. Fletcher, M.D.	Trinity	President
J. N. Buchanan	Trinity	Secretary
E. M. Clark, M.A.	Trinity	Treasurer
Hon. C. F. Lyttelton	Trinity	Librarian
A. W. M. S. Griffin	Trinity	Auditor
M. C. Albright	Trinity	
V. G. Thew	Trinity Hall	
G. N. M. Bland	King's	
H. W. Priestley	Trinity	
E. G. Williams	Trinity	
T. Holland-Hibbert	Trinity	

Michaelmas 1909 *to Easter* 1910

W. M. Fletcher, M.D.	Trinity	President
A. W. M. S. Griffin	Trinity	Secretary
E. M. Clark, M.A.	Trinity	Treasurer
V. G. Thew	Trinity Hall	Librarian M. & L.
E. G. Williams	Trinity	Auditor
T. Holland-Hibbert	Trinity	
W. D. Gibbs	Trinity	
W. P. D. Clarke	King's	
M. Falcon	Pembroke	
J. F. Ireland	Trinity	

Michaelmas 1910 *to Easter* 1911

W. M. Fletcher, M.D.	Trinity	President
T. Holland-Hibbert	Trinity	Secretary
E. M. Clark, M.A.	Trinity	Treasurer
W. P. D. Clarke	King's	Librarian
M. Falcon	Pembroke	Auditor

Michaelmas 1910 *to Easter* 1911 (*cont.*)

J. F. Ireland	Trinity
J. E. Murray-Smith	Magdalene
R. W. M. Arbuthnot	Trinity
A. O'N. C. Chichester	Trinity
J. A. M. Charles	Trinity

Michaelmas 1911 *to Easter* 1912

W. M. Fletcher, M.D.	Trinity	President
J. E. Murray-Smith	Magdalene	Secretary M.
E. M. Clark, M.A.	Trinity	Treasurer
R. W. M. Arbuthnot	Trinity	Librarian M., Secretary L. & E.
J. A. M. Charles	Trinity	Auditor
G. W. V. Hopley	Trinity	
C. W. Norman	Trinity	
B. B. Buckley	King's	
Hon. H. G. H. Mulholland	Trinity	
G. W. Barclay	Trinity Hall	
Hon. A. A. Tennyson	Trinity	
A. H. Lang	Trinity	

Michaelmas 1912 *to Easter* 1913

W. M. Fletcher, M.D.	Trinity	President
Hon. H. G. H. Mulholland	Trinity	Secretary
E. M. Clark, M.A.	Trinity	Treasurer
G. W. V. Hopley	Trinity	Librarian
C. W. Norman	Trinity	
G. W. Barclay	Trinity Hall	
C. R. le Blanc Smith	Trinity	
Hon. A. A. Tennyson	Trinity	
B. B. Buckley	King's	
A. H. Lang	Trinity	

Michaelmas 1913 *to Easter* 1914

W. M. Fletcher, M.D.	Trinity	President
G. W. V. Hopley	Trinity	Secretary
E. M. Clark, M.A.	Trinity	Treasurer
Hon. G. J. Mulholland	Trinity	Librarian
I. M. Hedley	King's	Auditor
G. L. Davies	Trinity	
K. S. M. Gladstone	Trinity Hall	
L. W. Lloyd	Clare	
D. L. Harvey	Trinity	
C. E. V. Buxton	Trinity	

Michaelmas 1914 *to Easter* 1915

S. Gaselee, M.A.	Magdalene	President
R. R. Sedgwick	Trinity	Secretary
E. M. Clark, M.A.	Trinity	Treasurer
L. Gjers	Trinity	
R. Courthope	Magdalene	
J. B. Heaton	Trinity	
G. Wilson	Trinity	

Michaelmas 1915 *to Michaelmas* 1917

S. Gaselee, M.A.	Magdalene	President
R. R. Sedgwick	Trinity	Secretary
E. M. Clark, M.A.	Trinity	Treasurer

The Club was closed from the end of the Michaelmas Term 1917 until the Michaelmas Term 1918.

Michaelmas 1918

S. Gaselee, M.A., C.B.E.	Magdalene	President
E. M. Clark, M.A.	Trinity	Treasurer
Temporary members:		
A. H. Marshall	Trinity	Secretary
W. Durnford	King's	
G. T. Lapsley	Trinity	

Lent and Easter 1919

S. Gaselee, M.A., C.B.E.	Magdalene	President
Sir Walter Durnford, G.B.E.	King's	Deputy President
Major C. E. V. Buxton	Trinity	Secretary
E. M. Clark, M.A.	Trinity	Treasurer
G. T. Lapsley, M.A.	Trinity	
M. Woosnam	Trinity	
G. Parker-Jervis	Magdalene	
G. M. Butler	Trinity	
P. I. Pease	Trinity	

Michaelmas 1919 *to Easter* 1920

S. Gaselee, M.A., C.B.E.	Magdalene	President M.
G. K. Dunning	Trinity	Secretary
E. M. Clark, M.A., O.B.E.	Trinity	Treasurer M., President L. & E.
G. Wilson	Trinity	Librarian
A. Swann	Trinity Hall	Auditor
R. H. Parker, M.A., M.C.	Trinity	Treasurer L. & E.

98

Michaelmas 1919 *to Easter* 1920 *(cont.)*

G. Parker-Jervis	Magdalene
G. M. Butler	Trinity
P. I. Pease	Trinity
K. S. M. Gladstone	Trinity Hall
H. G. C. Streatfeild	King's
H. Peake	Trinity

Michaelmas 1920 *to Easter* 1921

E. M. Clark, M.A., O.B.E.	Trinity	President
G. K. Dunning, B.A.	Trinity	Secretary M. & L.
R. H. Parker, M.A., M.C.	Trinity	Treasurer
A. D. B. Pearson	Trinity	Librarian M. & L., Secretary E.
G. Ashton	Trinity	Auditor
G. G. Phillips	Trinity	Librarian E.
G. M. Butler	Trinity	
H. Peake	Trinity	
J. H. Leycester	Magdalene	
T. M. Nussey	King's	
M. H. Scott	Christ's	
Hon. J. W. H. Fremantle	Trinity	

Michaelmas 1921 *to Easter* 1922

E. M. Clark, M.A., O.B.E.	Trinity	President
A. D. B. Pearson, B.A.	Trinity	Secretary
R. H. Parker, M.A., M.C.	Trinity	Treasurer
G. G. Phillips	Trinity	Librarian
Hon. J. W. H. Fremantle, B.A.	Trinity	Auditor
G. M. Butler	Trinity	
J. H. Leycester	Magdalene	
M. H. Scott	Christ's	
C. T. Ashton	Trinity	
W. H. Whitbread	Corpus Christi	
R. S. Nettleton	King's	

Michaelmas 1922 *to Easter* 1923

E. M. Clark, M.A., O.B.E.	Trinity	President
G. G. Phillips	Trinity	Secretary M. & L.
R. H. Parker, M.A., M.C.	Trinity	Treasurer
R. S. Nettleton	King's	Librarian M.
C. T. Ashton	Trinity	Auditor
I. Spencer	Trinity	Librarian L. & E.
R. H. Studholme	Trinity	Secretary E.
W. H. Whitbread	Corpus Christi	
F. J. W. Seely	Trinity	

Michaelmas 1922 *to Easter* 1923 *(cont.)*

L. R. W. de F. Mackeson King's
R. C. Huband Pembroke
A. L. Barclay Trinity
A. R. Gray Trinity

Michaelmas 1923 *to Easter* 1924

E. M. Clark, M.A., O.B.E.	Trinity	President
R. H. Studholme, B.A.	Trinity	Secretary
R. H. Parker, M.A., M.C.	Trinity	Treasurer
I. Spencer	Trinity	Librarian
R. C. Huband	Pembroke	Auditor
F. J. W. Seely	Trinity	
A. L. Barclay	Trinity	
A. R. Graham-Campbell	King's	
R. A. Pearson	Trinity Hall	
W. F. Smith	Trinity	
W. E. Seely	Trinity	

Michaelmas 1924 *to Easter* 1925

E. M. Clark, M.A., O.B.E.	Trinity	President
W. F. Smith	Trinity	Secretary
R. H. Parker, M.A., M.C.	Trinity	Treasurer
A. R. Graham-Campbell	King's	Librarian
A. L. Barclay	Trinity	Auditor
W. E. Anderson	Trinity	
R. G. Fielden	Magdalene	
W. J. Keswick	Trinity	
R. E. Morrison	Trinity	
R. C. Smith-Bingham	Trinity	

Michaelmas 1925 *to Easter* 1926

E. M. Clark, M.A., O.B.E.	Trinity	President
W. F. Smith	Trinity	Secretary M. & L.
R. H. Parker, M.A., M.C.	Trinity	Treasurer
C. G. Blaxter	St John's	Librarian
R. G. Fielden	Magdalene	Auditor M. & L., Secretary E.
R. C. Smith-Bingham	Trinity	
E. C. Hamilton Russel	Trinity	
Hon. J. S. Maclay	Trinity	
R. C. Parker	Trinity	
F. B. Dunbar-Kilburn	Trinity	
F. C. Pierce Grove	Trinity	
Lord Burghley	Magdalene	

100

Michaelmas 1926 to Easter 1927

E. M. Clark, M.A., O.B.E.	Trinity	President
Hon. J. S. Maclay	Trinity	Secretary
R. H. Parker, M.A., M.C.	Trinity	Treasurer
A. W. Hill	Clare	Librarian
J. A. King	Trinity	Auditor
Lord Burghley	Magdalene	
J. Abel-Smith	Trinity	
F. C. Pierce Grove	Trinity	
P. A. Tritton	Trinity	
G. N. Waldegrave	Trinity	
D. P. G. Moseley	Pembroke	

Michaelmas 1927 to Easter 1928

E. M. Clark, M.A., O.B.E.	Trinity	President
P. A. Tritton	Trinity	Secretary
R. H. Parker, M.A., M.C.	Trinity	Treasurer
A. W. Hill	Clare	Librarian
J. H. Keswick	Trinity	Auditor
J. Abel-Smith	Trinity	
D. P. G. Moseley	Pembroke	
J. G. Morrison	Magdalene	
A. D. Bonham Carter	Magdalene	
M. G. H. Brown	Trinity	

Michaelmas 1928 to Easter 1929

E. M. Clark, M.A., O.B.E.	Trinity	President
A. D. Bonham Carter	Magdalene	Secretary
R. H. Parker, M.A., M.C.	Trinity	Treasurer
M. H. Warriner	Trinity	Librarian
T. A. Brocklebank	Trinity	Auditor
R. Beesly	Trinity	
J. G. S. Donaldson	Trinity	
H. B. Hardy	Trinity	
W. W. Hicks Beach	Magdalene	
Lord Willoughby d'Eresby	Magdalene	

Michaelmas 1929 to Easter 1930

E. M. Clark, M.A., O.B.E.	Trinity	President M.
T. A. Brocklebank	Trinity	Secretary
R. H. Parker, M.A., M.C.	Trinity	Treasurer
Rev. F. H. H. Clark, M.A.	Magdalene	President E. & L.
M. H. Warriner	Trinity	
J. C. Hurst	Trinity	
Hon. A. B. Mildmay	Trinity	

101

P. W. Paget   Trinity
S. M. Pilkington   Trinity
F. J. R. Coleridge   Magdalene
Hon. R. Frankland   Pembroke

Michaelmas 1930 *to Easter* 1931

Rev. F. H. H. Clark, M.A.	Magdalene	President
F. J. R. Coleridge	Magdalene	Secretary
R. H. Parker, M.A., M.C.	Trinity	Treasurer
Hon. A. E. J. Bulwer-Lytton	Trinity	Librarian
T. A. Brocklebank	Trinity	Auditor M. & L.
R. H. Bull	Trinity	Auditor E.
K. C. Gandar-Dower	Trinity	
R. Hoare	Trinity	
Hon. P. Pleydell-Bouverie	Trinity	
Viscount Somerton	Trinity	
G. R. Hamilton	Magdalene	

Michaelmas 1931 *to Easter* 1932

Rev. F. H. H. Clark, M.A.	Magdalene	President
R. H. Bull	Trinity	Secretary
R. H. Parker, M.A., M.C.	Trinity	Treasurer
Sir J. F. Nicholson	Trinity	Librarian
G. R. Hamilton	Magdalene	Auditor
A. G. Hazlerigg	Trinity	
W. J. Stirling	Trinity	
K. S. Urquhart	Trinity	
T. C. S. Haywood	Magdalene	
C. M. Fletcher	Trinity	

Michaelmas 1932 *to Easter* 1933

Rev. F. H. H. Clark, M.A.	Magdalene	President
C. M. Fletcher	Trinity	Secretary
R. H. Parker, M.A., M.C.	Trinity	Treasurer M. & L.
Hon. C. S. Phillimore	Trinity	Librarian
R. H. Bull, B.A.	Trinity	Auditor
E. F. Collingwood, Ph.D.	Trinity	Treasurer E.
E. J. B. Nelson	Trinity	
S. C. Elworthy	Trinity	
Baron T. E. Dimsdale	Magdalene	
M. S. Gosling	Magdalene	
A. S. Lawrence	Trinity Hall	

Michaelmas 1933 to Easter 1934

Rev. F. H. H. Clark, M.A.	Magdalene	President
C. M. Fletcher, B.A.	Trinity	Secretary M.
E. F. Collingwood, Ph.D.	Trinity	Treasurer
D. J. Graham-Campbell	Trinity	Librarian M., Secretary L. & E.
M. S. Gosling	Magdalene	Auditor
M. Wilson	Trinity	Librarian L. & E.
Hon. C. S. Phillimore	Trinity	
A. M. L. Ponsonby	Trinity	
J. D. P. Watney	Trinity	
S. Lycett Green	Magdalene	
T. F. Blackwell	Magdalene	

Michaelmas 1934 to Easter 1935

Rev. F. H. H. Clark, M.A.	Magdalene	President
M. Wilson	Trinity	Secretary
E. F. Collingwood, Ph.D.	Trinity	Treasurer
D. O. Beale	Trinity	Librarian
J. H. C. Powell	Trinity	Auditor
N. E. W. Baker	Trinity	
S. J. Cuthbert	Trinity	
C. P. R. Bowen-Colthurst	Magdalene	
J. R. Dimsdale	Magdalene	
S. D. Heywood	Emmanuel	
J. H. G. Nevill	Trinity	

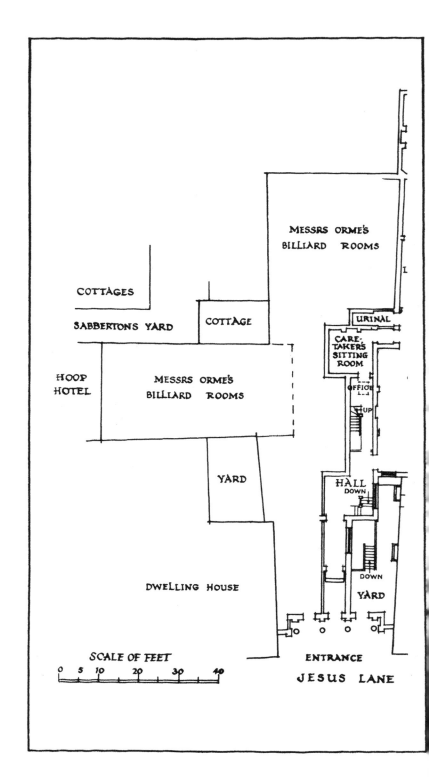

MESSRS ORME'S
BILLIARD ROOMS

COTTAGES

COTTAGE

SABBERTONS YARD

URINAL

CARE-
TAKER'S
SITTING
ROOM

HOOP
HOTEL

MESSRS ORME'S
BILLIARD ROOMS

OFFICE

UP

YARD

HALL
DOWN

DOWN

DWELLING HOUSE

YARD

SCALE OF FEET

0 5 10   20   30   40

ENTRANCE

JESUS LANE

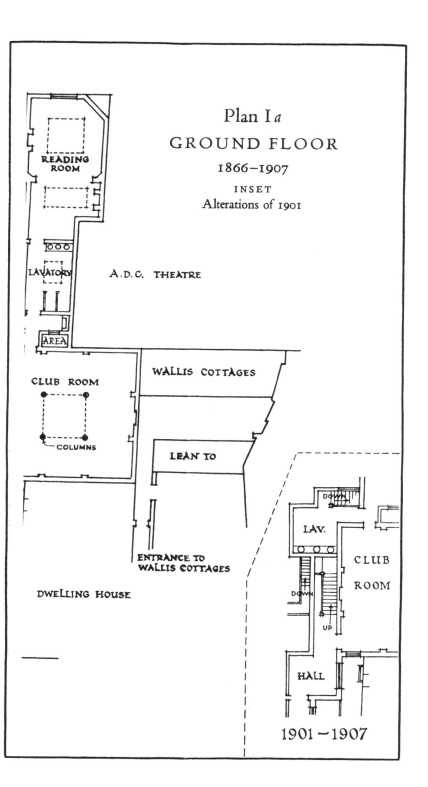

Plan I *a*

GROUND FLOOR

1866–1907

INSET
Alterations of 1901

READING ROOM

LAVATORY

A.D.C. THEATRE

AREA

CLUB ROOM

WALLIS COTTAGES

COLUMNS

LEAN TO

ENTRANCE TO WALLIS COTTAGES

DWELLING HOUSE

DOWN

LAV.

CLUB ROOM

DOWN

UP

HALL

1901–1907

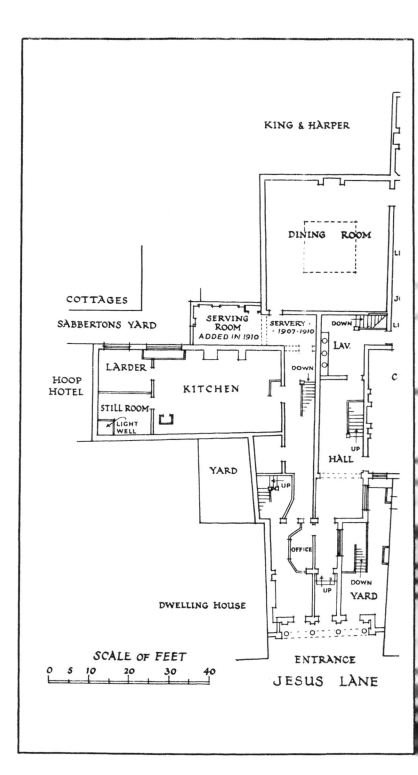

KING & HARPER

DINING ROOM

COTTAGES

SABBERTONS YARD

SERVING ROOM
ADDED IN 1910

SERVERY · 1907·1910

DOWN

LAV.

LARDER

HOOP HOTEL

KITCHEN

DOWN

STILL ROOM

LIGHT WELL

HALL

UP

YARD

UP

OFFICE

UP

DOWN

YARD

DWELLING HOUSE

SCALE OF FEET

0 5 10   20   30   40

ENTRANCE

JESUS LANE

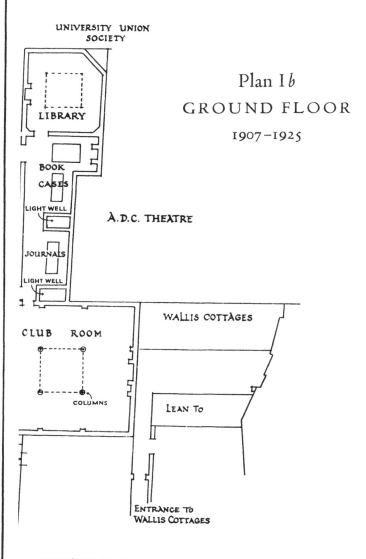

UNIVERSITY UNION
SOCIETY

LIBRARY

BOOK
CASES

LIGHT WELL

JOURNALS

LIGHT WELL

CLUB ROOM

COLUMNS

A.D.C. THEATRE

Plan I*b*

GROUND FLOOR

1907–1925

WALLIS COTTAGES

LEAN TO

ENTRANCE TO
WALLIS COTTAGES

DWELLING HOUSE

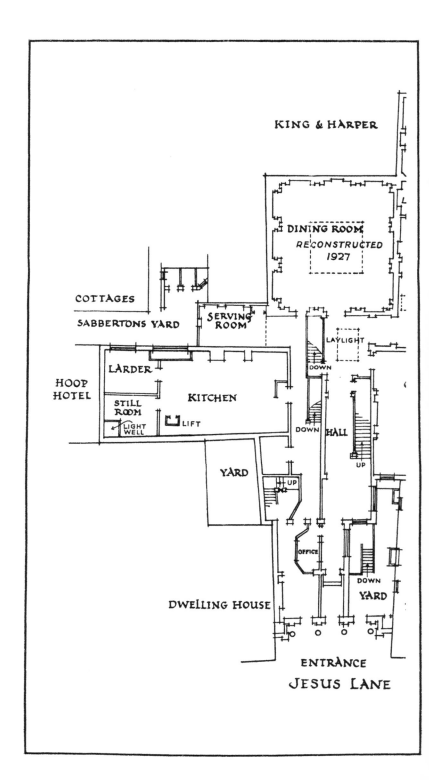

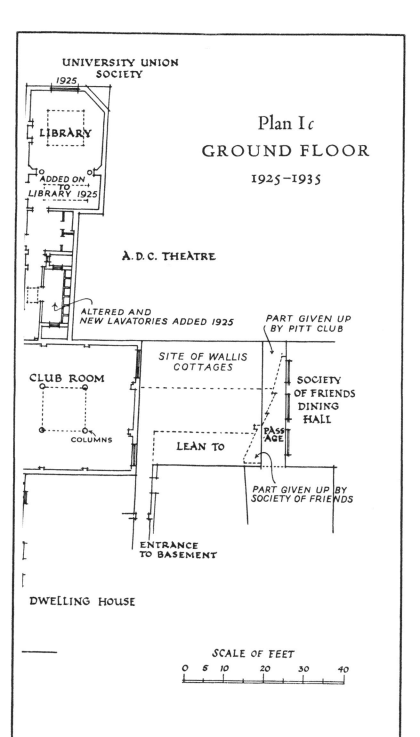

UNIVERSITY UNION
SOCIETY

1925

LIBRARY

○ ○
ADDED ON
TO
LIBRARY 1925

Plan I*c*

GROUND FLOOR

1925-1935

A. D. C. THEATRE

ALTERED AND
NEW LAVATORIES ADDED 1925

PART GIVEN UP
BY PITT CLUB

*SITE OF WALLIS
COTTAGES*

SOCIETY
OF FRIENDS
DINING
HALL

CLUB ROOM

○ ○

○ ○
COLUMNS

PASS-
AGE

LEAN TO

PART GIVEN UP BY
SOCIETY OF FRIENDS

ENTRANCE
TO BASEMENT

DWELLING HOUSE

SCALE OF FEET

0   5   10   20   30   40

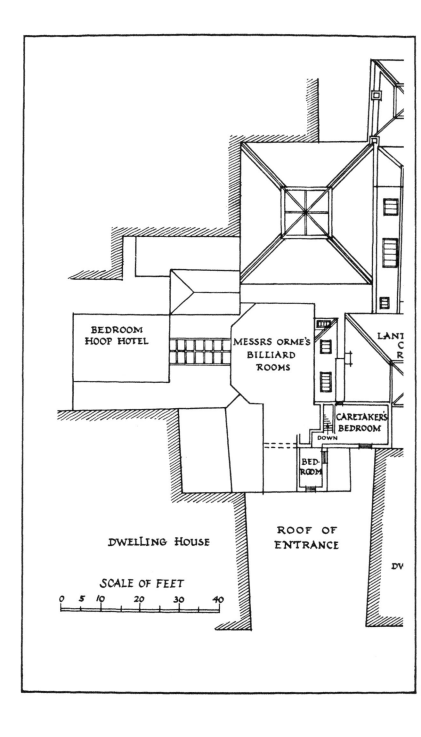

BEDROOM
HOOP HOTEL

MESSRS ORME'S
BILLIARD
ROOMS

LANT
C
R

CARETAKER'S
BEDROOM

DOWN

BED-
ROOM

ROOF OF
ENTRANCE

DWELLING HOUSE

DV

SCALE OF FEET

0   5   10   20   30   40

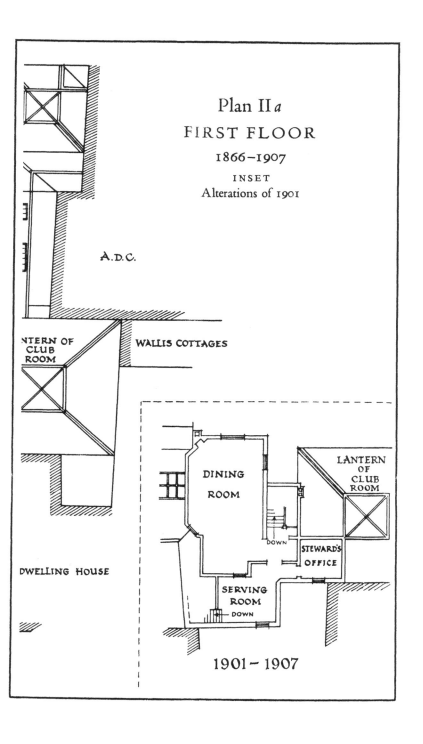

Plan II *a*

FIRST FLOOR

1866–1907

INSET
Alterations of 1901

A.D.C.

NTERN OF
CLUB
ROOM

WALLIS COTTAGES

LANTERN
OF
CLUB
ROOM

DINING
ROOM

DOWN

STEWARD'S
OFFICE

DWELLING HOUSE

SERVING
ROOM

DOWN

1901–1907

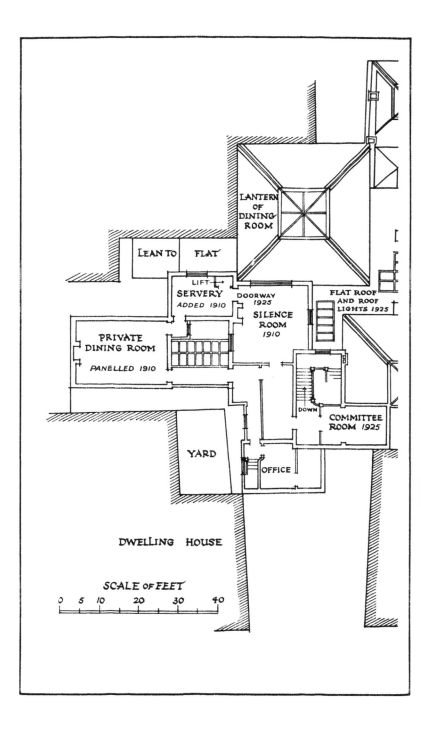

LANTERN
OF
DINING
ROOM

LEAN TO   FLAT

LIFT
SERVERY
ADDED 1910

DOORWAY
1925

FLAT ROOF
AND ROOF
LIGHTS 1925

SILENCE
ROOM
1910

PRIVATE
DINING ROOM

PANELLED 1910

DOWN

COMMITTEE
ROOM 1925

YARD

OFFICE

DWELLING   HOUSE

SCALE OF FEET

0   5 10   20   30   40

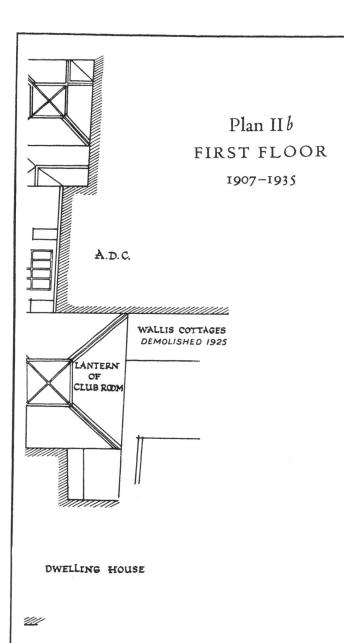

Plan II*b*

FIRST FLOOR

1907–1935

A.D.C.

WALLIS COTTAGES
DEMOLISHED 1925

LANTERN
OF
CLUB ROOM

DWELLING HOUSE